# SPIRITUAL SELF CARE MASTERY FOR BLACK WOMEN

## A COMPREHENSIVE WORKBOOK FOR PERSONAL GROWTH, AND EMPOWERMENT TO UNLOCK YOUR POWER, RECLAIM YOUR LIFE, AND EMBRACE ABUNDANCE WITH UNSTOPPABLE CONFIDENCE

### JADA AMARI

# CONTENTS

ISBN: 978-1-953149-51-0
Published by: Jada Amari
© Copyright 2024 - All rights reserved.

- **Unlocking Divine Connections:** A Practical Workbook Featuring Activities, Prompts, and Meditations to Cultivate Your Intuition and Deepen Your Spiritual Connection with Angel Guides

- **Entrepreneurship 101 for Black Women:** A Step-by-Step Guide to Launching, Growing, and Balancing Your Dream Business

- **Mindful Eating for Black Women:** A Guide to Nourishing Your Body and Mind

Scan me

Join a movement of Black women who are determined to achieve greatness and help others do the same. From daily habits and self-care routines to career advice and financial literacy, we've got you covered.

**Scan Me**

# INTRODUCTION

*"Your life is a sacred journey. It is about change, growth, discovery, movement, transformation, continuously expanding your vision of what is possible, stretching your soul, learning to see clearly and deeply, listening to your intuition, taking courageous challenges at every step along the way." – Caroline Adams*

Let me ask you a question: have you ever felt like there's more to life than what you're experiencing right now? Have you ever felt like you're on a never-ending rollercoaster of emotions and all you want is to finally find peace and balance? Well, you're not alone! As Black women, we face unique challenges that can often leave us feeling exhausted and disoriented.

What if I told you that the key to unlocking your full potential and living your best life is already within you, waiting to be discovered

Now, I know what you're thinking: "Jada, you don't know my life!" But trust me, I've been there. I've felt the weight of the world on my shoulders, trying to balance work, family, and everything in between, all while trying to find my place in this world. But you know what I realized? It's all about taking care of ourselves, from the inside out. And that starts with spiritual self-care.

You see, spiritual self-care is the foundation for personal growth, empowerment, and an unstoppable, confident life. It's about nurturing our inner power and potential to help us rise above the challenges that come our way. And this, my friend, is the journey we're about to embark on together.

Imagine waking up each day with a renewed sense of purpose, inner peace, and confidence, knowing that you have the tools to navigate life's ups and downs. Picture yourself surrounded by a tribe of supportive, like-minded women who uplift and inspire you. That's the kind of life you deserve, and that's the life you'll find in these pages.

Now, you might be wondering, "Why should I listen to Jada?" Well, let me tell you a little bit about myself. I've been on my own spiritual journey for years, diving deep into self-care practices, seeking guidance from mentors, and even becoming a certified life coach. I've seen firsthand the power of spiritual self-care and how it can transform lives, including my own. And, I'm passionate about sharing these life-changing tools with my fellow Black women!

In the chapters that follow, you'll explore various aspects of spiritual self-care such as soul awakening, heartfelt healing, gratitude, mindfulness, intention-setting, yoga, journaling, affirmations, connecting with nature and your tribe, embracing your divine femininity, creating sacred spaces, and establishing consistent rituals and routines. Each chapter is designed to help you embrace your authentic self, while also equipping you with the tools you need to navigate life's challenges with grace and resilience.

I still remember the day when everything changed for my dear friend Keisha. She was sitting on her couch, tears streaming down her face, feeling utterly defeated. It felt like the world was crumbling around her; her job was stressing her out, her relationships were falling apart, and she couldn't remember the last time she felt genuinely happy. She was lost, tired, and at her wit's end.

That's when her wise grandma called her out of the blue. She had this uncanny way of knowing when something was off, even from miles away. As Keisha tearfully poured her heart out to her, her grandma listened intently and then shared a piece of wisdom that has stuck with her ever since: "Baby girl, when life gets tough, remember that you have everything you need within you to rise above it all. You just have to believe in yourself and take care of your spirit."

Something about her grandma's words resonated deep within Keisha. It was like a lightbulb went off in her head, and she realized that she'd been neglecting her own spiritual health. She had been so focused on trying to please others and juggling all her responsibilities that she had forgotten to nourish her own soul. It was time for a change.

That conversation with her grandma sparked the beginning of Keisha's spiritual self-care journey. She started to explore different practices, sought guidance from mentors, and surrounded herself with like-minded women who uplifted and supported her. Slowly, she began to rediscover her inner power and purpose. Her life transformed, and she found the peace, balance, and confidence she had been craving for so long.

This story is not just about Keisha, but a shared experience among many Black women who are searching for that inner light amid life's chaos.

Keisha's story is a testament to the power of spiritual self-care and the incredible transformation that can happen when we invest in ourselves. Her journey shows us that no matter how tough life gets, embracing our inner power and nurturing our spirits can help us rise above any challenge and achieve our dreams.

It is my hope that by sharing her journey and the tools she's learned along the way, we can come together and empower one another to embrace our true selves and unlock our unlimited potential.

Alright, it's time to kick off this life-changing journey to your unstoppable self.

Are you prepared to unlock your power and embrace your authentic self? Are you eager to plunge into the world of spiritual self-care and unearth the secrets to a balanced, abundant, and self-assured life?

If your answer is a resounding yes, then take a deep breath, have faith in yourself, and let's leap into this adventure hand in hand! Together we'll explore the unknown, conquer our fears, and rise like the radiant queens we are, all while staying true to ourselves and shining our brightest.

So, turn the page, and let's embark on this transformation together, one fabulous step at a time. Remember - you are powerful, you are capable, and you deserve to live a life overflowing with abundance, joy, and unstoppable confidence.

# CHAPTER 1

# DISCOVERING YOUR SPIRITUAL ESSENCE

*"A woman in harmony with her spirit is like a river flowing. She goes where she will without pretense and arrives at her destination prepared to be herself and only herself." - Maya Angelou*

G irl, have you ever sensed a deeper connection whispering your name, urging you to answer its call? Trust me, you're not alone! In this chapter, we're going to unveil the power of spirituality as a self-care tool to help you find balance and strength to conquer life's challenges. So, get ready to awaken your soul and embrace the magic that lies within.

There are times when life feels like an endless grind, making it easy for us to lose touch with our true purpose. Amidst the hustle and bustle of daily life, our spiritual essence can become obscured, leaving us feeling disconnected. But here's the thing: spirituality is essential for self-care and personal growth. It's what makes you unique and infuses your life with meaning.

Together we'll uncover the transformative role of spirituality in our lives, discussing its essence and learning how to tap into that powerful force. We'll also explore the delicate art of balancing our spiritual practice with the demands of daily life, ensuring that we remain grounded and present without neglecting other important aspects of our journey. Through this exploration, we'll discover the magic of connecting with our spiritual selves, empowering us to rise above challenges and live a life infused with purpose and passion.

## DEFINING SPIRITUALITY AND ITS ROLE IN SELF-CARE

When you think about self-care, you might picture bubble baths and spa days, but it goes much deeper than that. True self-care involves nourishing your soul, and that's where spirituality comes in. But what is spirituality, and why is it so important for Black women like us?

Well, spirituality is a deeply personal experience. It is like having a one-on-one conversation with something way bigger than ourselves, whether that's God, the universe, or simply the energy that connects us all. Spirituality is about finding meaning and purpose in our lives, and it plays a crucial role in our overall well-being.

As Black women, we face unique obstacles in our daily lives. From systemic racism to gender inequality, there's no shortage of stressors. But by tapping into our spirituality, we can find the strength and resilience to rise above these challenges. We can use our spiritual practices to recharge, refocus, and reclaim our power. So, let's dive into some ways to define and embrace spirituality in our self-care routine.

One way to approach spirituality is through religious practices. For many of us, our faith is a significant source of comfort and guidance. Whether you're attending church services, praying, or studying sacred texts, these practices can help strengthen your spiritual connection and provide a sense of belonging. Don't be afraid to explore different faiths and beliefs to find what resonates with you.

But spirituality isn't limited to religion. You can also explore non-religious practices, like meditation, yoga, or mindfulness. These practices can help you tune into your inner self and foster a deeper connection with the world around you. I remember when I first tried meditation, I was skeptical. But as I sat there, focusing on my breath, I began to feel a sense of calm and clarity that I had never experienced before.

And let's not forget the power of nature. Simply spending time in the great outdoors can awaken our spiritual side. Whether you're walking through a park, hiking up a mountain, or watching the sunset, connecting with nature can remind us of our place in the grand scheme of things. So, take a moment to appreciate the beauty around you and let it nourish your soul.

I know that incorporating spirituality into your self-care routine might seem overwhelming at first, but remember: It's all about finding what works for you. You don't have to do it all – just start with one practice that speaks to your soul and see where it takes you.

As you explore your spiritual side, remember to give yourself grace. Your spiritual journey is unique to you, and there's no right or wrong way to go about it. And hey, if you stumble along the way, just remember that even the most enlightened among us have bad days.

I have to admit, once I started embracing my spiritual side, everything changed for the better. I felt more centered, more connected, and more empowered to face life's challenges head-on.

Now that we've laid the groundwork for defining spirituality and its role in self-care, it's time to dive into the next step: tapping into your spiritual essence.

## HOW TO TAP INTO YOUR SPIRITUAL ESSENCE

Finding and nurturing that divine spark within you is essential for personal growth and empowerment, sis. But how do you get started? Here's a step-by-step guide to help you tap into your spiritual essence and transform your life.

**Create a sacred space:** To tap into your spiritual essence, you need a space where you can connect with your inner self, uninterrupted. This could be a quiet corner in your home, a spot in your garden, or even your favorite comfy chair. Fill this space with items that inspire and uplift you – think candles, crystals, or pictures of loved ones. When you're in this space, you're telling your soul, "It's time to connect, girl!"

**Establish a daily practice:** Consistency is key when it comes to connecting with your spiritual essence. Set aside some time each day for prayer, meditation, journaling, or any other spiritual practice that resonates with you. This is your time to tune in and listen to your soul's wisdom.

**Embrace self-love:** You can't tap into your spiritual essence if you're constantly tearing yourself down. Start cultivating self-love by speaking kindly to yourself, celebrating your accomplishments, and honoring your body. Remember, you are a queen, and you deserve to be treated as such!

**Listen to your intuition:** Your intuition is your soul's GPS, guiding you on the path to personal growth and empowerment. Learn to trust your gut feeling and pay attention to any recurring thoughts or patterns. They might be clues from your spiritual essence, leading you to your true purpose.

**Connect with your ancestors:** As Black women, our roots run deep and our ancestors' strength and resilience flow through us. Connecting with your ancestors can help you tap into your spiritual essence and unlock your power. Set up an ancestral altar or try meditating on their wisdom and guidance.

**Find your tribe:** Surrounding yourself with like-minded, supportive people is essential for spiritual growth. Reach out to friends, join a spiritual community, or attend workshops and retreats to connect with others who share your spiritual journey.

**Keep learning and growing:** Your spiritual essence is like a muscle – the more you work it, the stronger it becomes. Keep seeking knowledge, attending workshops, or reading books on spirituality to continue growing and deepening your connection with your spiritual essence.

**Practice gratitude:** Focusing on the blessings in your life helps you cultivate a positive mindset and connect with your spiritual essence. Start each day by listing three things you're grateful for – it's a game-changer, I promise.

**Be open to the journey:** Your spiritual journey is unique and ever-evolving, just like you. Be open to change, and trust that the universe has your back. Embrace the twists and turns, knowing that they're all part of the divine plan.

**Reflect on your progress:** As you tap into your spiritual essence, take time to reflect on your growth and the changes you've experienced. What challenges have you overcome? How have your beliefs and values shifted? Use these insights to guide you on your path to spiritual self-care mastery.

Let me share a story about my friend, Tasha; a beautiful, vibrant, and successful Black woman who seemed to have it all together – a great job, a loving family, and a supportive group of friends. But deep down, she was struggling with feelings of emptiness and disconnection, like she was missing something essential in her life.

One day, Tasha confided in me about these feelings, and I suggested that she might be missing a connection to her spiritual essence. At first she was skeptical, but she decided to give it a shot. What did she have to lose, right?

She started by creating a sacred space in her home. She filled it with items that brought her joy and peace – beautiful African art, a plush meditation cushion, and aromatic incense. This space became her sanctuary, a place where she could relax, unwind, and connect with her inner self.

Next, Tasha began exploring different spiritual practices. She tried meditation, journaling, and even yoga. She discovered that she loved the stillness and introspection that meditation provided, so she committed to a daily practice. Every morning, before the hustle and bustle of the day, she would sit in her sacred space and meditate, focusing on her breath and the sensations in her body.

As her meditation practice deepened, she started to notice subtle changes in her life. She was more patient, more compassionate, and more in tune with her intuition. She began to trust herself and her inner wisdom, making decisions that aligned with her values and desires.

Inspired by her progress, she decided to delve even deeper into her spiritual journey. She attended workshops and retreats, connecting with other Black women on a similar path. She formed a sister circle, a group of like-minded women who met regularly to support each other in their spiritual growth.

Over time, Tasha began to honor her ancestors by incorporating ancestral reverence into her spiritual practice. She set up an altar in her sacred space, displaying photographs of her ancestors and offering them water, flowers, and food. This connection to her roots gave her strength and a deeper sense of belonging.

Slowly but surely, she felt more fulfilled and connected to her spiritual essence. The emptiness she once felt was replaced with a sense of purpose and a newfound appreciation for her unique journey as a Black woman.

Tasha's story is a testament to the power of tapping into one's spiritual essence. By committing to her spiritual journey, she transformed her life, embracing her power and reclaiming her sense of self. And if Tasha can do it, so can you.

By following the above steps, just like Tasha, you'll be well on your way to tapping into your spiritual essence, unlocking your power, and reclaiming your life. But remember, this is just the beginning. The journey to spiritual self-care mastery doesn't stop here. The next challenge? Balancing spirituality and everyday life.

## BALANCING SPIRITUALITY AND EVERYDAY LIFE

Now that we've explored tapping into your spiritual essence, let's explore how to balance your spiritual life with your everyday hustle. I know it's not always easy for us Black women to find that sweet spot between our spiritual practice and the daily grind. But trust me, striking that balance is essential for personal growth and unstoppable confidence.

### 1. Prioritize your spiritual practice

You know what they say, "You can't pour from an empty cup." So, make your spiritual practice a priority. Schedule time for meditation, prayer, or yoga, just like you would any other appointment. If you're a morning person, start your day with a calming ritual. If evenings work better, wind down with a relaxing spiritual routine. Remember, consistency is key to reaping the benefits of spiritual self-care.

## 2. Set boundaries

Set boundaries to protect your spiritual practice. Say no to things that drain your energy and make space for activities that nourish your soul. Communicate your needs to loved ones and be firm about your commitments. Your spiritual growth is just as important as anything else in your life, and it's time to treat it that way.

## 3. Integrate spirituality into your daily life

Who says spirituality has to be confined to a specific time or place? Practice mindfulness throughout your day, whether you're at work or running errands. Bring a sense of gratitude and presence to each task, and you'll find that even mundane chores become sacred moments.

## 4. Build a support system

Connect with like-minded sisters who share your spiritual values. Create a safe space where you can discuss your spiritual journey, exchange insights, and uplift each other. There's nothing like the power of sisterhood to keep you grounded and motivated.

## 5. Keep it real

Don't try to emulate someone else's spiritual journey. Your path is uniquely yours, and it's okay if it looks different from others'. Listen to your inner voice and honor your own needs, even if they don't fit the mold. Remember, authenticity is at the heart of a fulfilling spiritual life.

## 6. Stay flexible

Life happens, and sometimes your spiritual routine may need to adapt to your circumstances. Be open to change and willing to modify your practice when needed. The key is staying connected to your spiritual essence, even when the world around you is shifting.

## 7. Practice forgiveness and let go of negativity

Holding onto grudges and negative emotions can weigh you down and affect your spiritual well-being. Practice forgiveness and release resentments to create space for love, peace, and spiritual growth. Remember, forgiving others is an act of self-love, and it frees you from the chains of negativity.

## 8. Stay grounded with spiritual reminders

Surround yourself with objects or symbols that remind you of your spiritual journey. This can include inspirational quotes, crystals, or spiritual artwork. These visual reminders can help you stay connected to your spiritual essence throughout the day and serve as touchstones to center you during challenging moments

## 9. Take breaks for spiritual recharge

Sometimes, you just need a breather to reconnect with your spiritual essence. Allow yourself mini breaks throughout the day to pause, reflect, and recharge. It could be as simple as a 5-minute meditation, a moment of silence, or a quick walk outside to reconnect with nature. These breaks can help you maintain your spiritual balance and keep you grounded amidst the chaos of everyday life.

Alright, it's time for some self-reflection. Grab your journal and take a moment to ponder these question

- How can you prioritize your spiritual practice in your daily life?
- What boundaries do you need to set to protect your spiritual growth?
- How can you integrate spirituality into your everyday activities?

Remember, you deserve a spiritual life that's vibrant, nourishing, and empowering. By finding a balance between your spiritual practice and your daily routine, you can unlock your power, reclaim your life, and embrace abundance with unstoppable confidence. Keep shining, beautiful soul!

## SUMMARY, ACTION STEPS & EXERCISES

- Set aside daily "me-time" for spiritual practice, whether it's meditation, prayer, or journaling. Consistency is key to deepening your connection with your inner self.
- Tune into your intuition by paying attention to your feelings, thoughts, and physical sensations. Trust the guidance that comes from within.
- Stay mindful of your spiritual practice throughout the day, finding little ways to stay connected; like taking deep breaths, practicing gratitude, or pausing for a moment of reflection.

---

We've been on a journey exploring the importance of spirituality in self-care and discovering how tapping into your spiritual essence can empower you along the way. Through this chapter, you've gained insights into what spirituality means and how to connect with your inner self. You've also learned how to weave spirituality into your daily routine to avoid burnout and maintain balance.

As you move forward, remember to be gentle with yourself and trust your intuition. Your spiritual journey is unique and ever-evolving. There will be times when you feel like you're on the right path, and other times when you feel lost. But know that it's all part of the journey and that you're exactly where you need to be.

Now that you've awakened your soul and connected with your spiritual essence, it's time to delve deeper into heartfelt healing. In the next chapter, we'll explore the power of forgiveness and letting go. Holding onto grudges and past hurts can hold you back from living your best life. But with heartfelt healing, you can release those negative emotions and move forward with a renewed sense of purpose.

Remember, your journey to spiritual self-care mastery isn't a sprint, it's a marathon. Keep reading to learn how to embrace forgiveness and let go of the past. Together, we'll continue to unlock your power, reclaim your life, and embrace abundance with unstoppable confidence.

# CHAPTER 2
# EMBRACING FORGIVENESS AND LETTING GO

"FORGIVENESS IS NOT AN OCCASIONAL ACT, IT IS A CONSTANT ATTITUDE." - MAYA ANGELOU

Picture this: you're walking down the street, and you're carrying a heavy suitcase filled with everything that's ever hurt or upset you. Sounds exhausting, right? That's what it's like when we hold onto grudges, resentment, and pain. The good news is that you can put that suitcase down! This chapter is all about embracing forgiveness, releasing emotional baggage, and moving on with grace and resilience. Trust me, once you master this, you'll feel like a whole new woman, ready to conquer the world and strut like the queen you are!

Forgiveness can sometimes feel like a foreign concept, especially when we've been wronged or hurt deeply. But, I'm here to tell you that it's not only possible but necessary for your emotional and spiritual well-being. When you forgive, you're not doing it for the other person; you're doing it for yourself. You're allowing yourself to heal, grow, and rise above the pain.

In this chapter, we're going to explore the power of forgiveness in self-care, the steps to release emotional baggage, and how to move on with grace and resilience. Through personal anecdotes, relatable examples, and practical advice, you'll discover how to let go of past hurts and embrace the healing process. This journey won't always be easy, but it will be life-changing.

## THE POWER OF FORGIVENESS IN SELF-CARE

As Black women, we're no strangers to the challenges life throws at us. With so many responsibilities and stressors, it's all too easy to cling to negative emotions and grudges. But let me tell you, holding onto these feelings only creates more tension and stress in our lives. Forgiveness and releasing emotional baggage are essential for our mental and emotional healing. It allows us to move forward with positivity, peace, and a lighter heart.

Starting on this journey of forgiveness, the first step is acknowledging our feelings. Recognizing and understanding our emotions is crucial before we can begin the process of forgiveness. Take some time to reflect on the situation and how it makes you feel. Writing it down in a journal can be incredibly helpful, like releasing a valve on a pressure cooker. For instance, let's say you have a falling out with a friend who said something hurtful. Instead of ignoring the hurt, write about how it made you feel and why it affected you. It's important to validate your emotions without judgment.

Once you've acknowledged your feelings, try practicing empathy. Put yourself in the other person's shoes and remember that everyone makes mistakes. For example, maybe your friend was going through a tough time and lashed out. By understanding their situation, it becomes easier to forgive. Alongside empathy, letting go of expectations is another powerful step in practicing forgiveness. We often hold onto grudges because others don't meet our expectations. Ask yourself if these expectations are realistic, and consider releasing them to help diffuse anger and resentment.

Focusing on the present moment is a game-changer. Instead of dwelling on the past, concentrate on what you can do now to improve your life. Shift your attention to the positive aspects of your world, and you'll find it easier to let go of negative emotions. As you do this, don't forget to prioritize self-care. Do things that make you happy and relaxed, whether it's reading a book, taking a bath, or going for a walk. By taking care of yourself, you create a supportive environment that encourages healing and forgiveness.

Surrounding yourself with positivity is another key component. Engage with positive people, activities, and environments that help maintain a radiant mindset and keep those negative vibes at bay. Remember, you deserve to be in uplifting spaces that nourish your soul. Seeking support is crucial, too. Don't be afraid to reach out to friends, family, or even a therapist. Sharing your emotions and experiences can be incredibly healing. Sometimes, just voicing your feelings can help release that emotional baggage.

Lastly, embrace an attitude of gratitude. Every day, focus on the positive things in your life and jot down three things you're thankful for. This practice can shift your perspective, making it easier to let go of emotional baggage and embrace forgiveness. By incorporating these steps into your daily life, you'll create a foundation for healing and growth, empowering you to live with more peace and abundance.

## STEPS TO EMBRACE SELF-FORGIVENESS

It's essential to remember that forgiving ourselves is just as important as forgiving others. Self-forgiveness is a powerful tool for healing, growth, and empowerment. Let's explore some ways to embrace self-forgiveness and become the best version of ourselves.

First, let's talk about acknowledging our feelings. When we make mistakes, it's normal to feel guilt or shame. Instead of sweeping these emotions under the rug, we need to face them head-on. For example, if you feel guilty about not being there for a friend during a tough time, recognize that guilt, and allow yourself to process it.

Journaling can be a helpful way to explore these emotions. Write about the situation and how it affected you. This can bring clarity and help you understand your feelings, paving the way for self-forgiveness.

Next, we need to practice self-compassion. Remind yourself that nobody's perfect, and we all make mistakes. Think about how you would treat a loved one who's struggling with self-forgiveness. Would you berate them, or would you show them kindness and understanding? Treat yourself with the same empathy and warmth.

For example, if you're blaming yourself for a failed relationship, remind yourself that relationships are a two-way street, and it's not solely your responsibility to make things work. Be gentle with yourself and remember that you deserve love and compassion.

Accepting responsibility for our actions is another crucial step. It's essential to be honest with ourselves about the part we played in any situation. By owning our actions, we can learn from them and grow. However, avoid falling into the trap of excessive self-blame. Recognize your responsibility, but also understand that there are always other factors at play.

Once you've acknowledged your role, it's time to make amends when possible. Apologize to those you've hurt or find ways to rectify the situation. For instance, if you neglected a friendship due to your busy schedule, reach out and let your friend know you're sorry and want to reconnect. This act can help mend relationships and, in turn, help you forgive yourself.

Learning from our mistakes is also essential. Reflect on what you can do differently in the future and make a conscious effort to grow. If you've noticed a pattern of behavior that led to negative outcomes, work on breaking that cycle. This could mean improving communication, setting boundaries, or seeking professional help.

Finally, let's focus on moving forward. Dwelling on the past won't change it, but we can take control of our present and future. Celebrate your progress and remind yourself that you're a work in progress. Shift your focus to the positive aspects of your life and the goals you want to achieve. When you're busy building a bright future, there's less room for guilt and regret.

## MOVING ON WITH GRACE AND RESILIENCE

I know it can be tough, but you're a strong, beautiful woman who's capable of facing any challenge. So, let's break it down into bite-sized pieces and get you feeling renewed, unburdened, and ready to embrace abundance!

Although we touched on this previously, it's important to mention I know forgiveness can be a hard pill to swallow. Sometimes, the people who hurt us most are the ones we love deeply, and forgiving them can feel like letting them off the hook. But, forgiveness is about freeing yourself, not them. When you choose to forgive, you're taking back your power and releasing that weight from your heart. So, give yourself permission to let go of grudges, resentment, and bitterness. You deserve to be free and live your best life!

Now, let's talk about finding closure. I'm not talking about getting back together with your ex or having that "one last conversation" with someone who hurt you. Nah, closure comes from within. It's about accepting the past and coming to terms with the fact that you can't change it. Take a moment to reflect on the lessons you've learned and how they've shaped you into the amazing woman you are today. It's time to let go of what's holding you back and embrace the future with open arms.

One way to move on gracefully is to cultivate resilience. Life will always throw curveballs at you, but it's how you deal with them that matters. And as a Black woman, you know a thing or two about resilience! It's part of our DNA, honey! So, tap into that strength, and remember that you have the power to overcome any obstacle. Surround yourself with positive, uplifting people who believe in you and your dreams. And when the going gets tough, remind yourself of all the challenges you've conquered and the incredible accomplishments you've achieved. You got this!

Now, I know it's easier said than done, but another important aspect of moving on is to stop dwelling on the past. Look, we've all had moments where we replay a conversation or an incident in our heads, wishing we'd said or done something differently. But you know what? That's not helping you grow. So, instead of living in the past, focus on the present and the amazing opportunities that lie ahead. Embrace the fact that you're a work in progress, and every day is a chance to learn, grow, and become a better version of yourself.

To help you embrace your inner resilience, take some time to self-reflect. Ask yourself, "What can I learn from this situation? How can I grow and become stronger because of it?"

This kind of introspection can help you identify patterns and habits that might be holding you back, so you can break free from them and step into your power.

## SUMMARY, ACTION STEPS & EXERCISES

- Set aside 10 minutes each day for quiet reflection, focusing on situations or people you need to forgive. Write down your feelings and thoughts, and say a forgiveness affirmation like, "I choose to release this pain and forgive."
- Create a "letting go" ritual: Find a quiet space, light a candle, and write down the emotional baggage you wish to release on a piece of paper. As you burn the paper, visualize the negative emotions dissolving and being replaced by a sense of peace and healing.
- Every morning, set an intention for the day to embrace change, maintain healthy boundaries, and cultivate a positive mindset. Keep a journal to track your progress and celebrate your achievements in moving forward with grace and resilience.

We explored the transformative power of forgiveness and its crucial role in self-care throughout this chapter. We've gone through how it can help you release emotional baggage, cultivate self-love, and move forward with grace and resilience. By embracing forgiveness, you're choosing to free yourself from the chains of past hurts and step into a life of healing, growth, and abundance.

Our next chapter will take you on a beautiful adventure into the world of gratitude. We'll uncover how embracing an attitude of thankfulness can bring more happiness, fulfillment, and abundance into your life. We'll also explore practical tips and techniques to make gratitude an essential part of your daily self-care routine.

So, let's keep this self-care party going, and join me in the next chapter. Together, we'll learn how to appreciate life's blessings and amplify the joy in our lives. Let's grow, thrive, and conquer the world with gratitude, one day at a time!

# CHAPTER 3
# HARNESSING THE POWER OF GRATITUDE

*"Gratitude makes sense of our past, brings peace for today, and creates a vision for tomorrow." - Melody Beattie*

Let me tell you about the game-changer in our self-care journey: gratitude. Embracing an attitude of gratitude can unlock a positive mindset, improve mental well-being, and open the door to new opportunities and blessings.

In this chapter, we'll start by uncovering the transformative impact of gratitude. When you practice gratitude, you'll notice a shift in your mindset and overall mental well-being. It's like flipping a switch and turning on the lights in a dark room. We'll discuss how a thankful heart can lead to a more positive outlook on life, improved relationships, and a stronger sense of self-worth. Next, we'll move on to creating a gratitude practice. Just like any other skill, gratitude needs consistent practice to make a lasting impact on our lives.

Together, we'll explore various techniques to incorporate gratitude into your daily routine. From journaling to meditation, there's a gratitude practice for every queen out there. By committing to a regular practice, we can reflect on life's blessings and strengthen our connections with loved ones. Lastly, we'll delve into the magic of attracting abundance through thankfulness. When you express gratitude, it's like sending out a signal to the universe, telling it that you're ready to receive more blessings. We'll discuss how an attitude of gratitude can manifest more abundance in all areas of our lives, from relationships to career opportunities, and even our finances.

Ready to harness the power of gratitude and change your life for the better? Let's explore how thankfulness can transform your world!

## THE TRANSFORMATIVE IMPACT OF GRATITUDE

Gratitude has a transformative impact on our lives, especially when it feels like the world is weighing us down. In those moments, it's crucial to remember the power of gratitude, which can help shift our focus from the negative to the positive. By practicing gratitude, we can change our lives from the inside out, and find strength even in the face of adversity.

Black women, in particular, face unique challenges such as microaggressions, systemic inequalities, and everyday stressors. Microaggressions can show up in comments like, "You're so well-spoken," implying surprise at their eloquence. Systemic inequalities manifest in various ways, like pay disparities and limited career opportunities at work. Additionally, everyday stressors include the pressure to balance work and family life, as well as navigating racial stereotypes.

Despite these challenges, embracing gratitude can be a powerful way to foster resilience and maintain a healthy perspective. By being grateful for our accomplishments, the support of loved ones, and the opportunities that come our way, we can empower ourselves and cultivate emotional well-being. In the face of adversity, gratitude shines a light on the positive aspects of life and encourages us to keep pushing forward.

Gratitude can work wonders on our mental and emotional well-being. When we make a habit of practicing gratitude, our brains rewire themselves to highlight the positive aspects of our lives, leaving us feeling happier and more content. Let me share a little snippet of my own journey with you.

There was a time when I found myself going through a particularly rough patch. I was feeling down, and it seemed like life just wasn't going my way. I was struggling with work, my relationships were strained, and my self-esteem had taken a serious hit. In the midst of this turmoil, I decided to try something different – I started focusing on the things I was grateful for in my life.

Each day, I made a point of counting my blessings, whether it was appreciating a good conversation with a friend, enjoying a hearty meal, or simply taking a moment to breathe in the fresh air. As I began to acknowledge and appreciate these small joys, I noticed a profound shift in my perspective. The clouds that had been hanging over my life started to part, revealing a brighter outlook.

As I continued to practice gratitude, I became more aware of the love and support that surrounded me. I started to see the opportunities for growth and self-improvement that had been hidden in the challenges I faced. My relationships began to heal, and I found myself more motivated and focused at work.

This experience taught me that even in the darkest moments, gratitude can be a beacon of light guiding us towards a happier, more fulfilled life.

Another transformational aspect of gratitude is its ability to strengthen our relationships. When we genuinely appreciate and express gratitude to our friends, family, and even co-workers, we nurture our connections and foster a sense of belonging. Like that time I told my best friend how much I cherished her support during a challenging period. Our bond grew stronger than ever, and we became each other's rock.

Gratitude can also help us navigate and overcome adversity. As Black women, this adversity can feel insurmountable. But by focusing on the things we're grateful for, we build resilience and create a sense of perspective that helps us cope with life's ups and downs. Remember, we've been through a lot, but we always come out stronger.

Let's go over the importance of self-reflection and introspection in practicing gratitude. Ask yourself, "What am I truly grateful for today?" Take a moment to ponder that question and feel the warmth of gratitude in your heart. By digging deep and exploring our own beliefs and values, we promote personal growth and self-awareness.

As you can see, the transformative impact of gratitude is undeniable. Gratitude can improve our mental health, strengthen relationships, and help us overcome adversity. As Black women, embracing gratitude is not just an act of self-care; it's an act of self-love and empowerment.

## CREATING A GRATITUDE PRACTICE

Now that we spoke about the transformative impact of gratitude, let's explore how to create a gratitude practice tailored to our unique experiences as Black women. Just like anything worth having, cultivating gratitude takes time, consistency, and dedication. But trust me, the rewards are well worth the effort.

First, let's talk about gratitude journaling. This practice is all about taking a few moments each day to jot down the things you're grateful for. It can be big or small, from the laughter shared with friends to the warmth of the sun on your face. Don't be afraid to get creative and make your gratitude journal a reflection of your beautiful, vibrant self. Decorate it with inspiring quotes, affirmations, or even pictures that remind you of your blessings. And remember, consistency is key, so try to set aside a specific time each day to write in your journal. Before you know it, gratitude will become second nature.

Another powerful practice is gratitude meditation. Find a quiet space where you can sit comfortably and close your eyes. Take a few deep breaths, inhaling positivity and exhaling negativity. Now, visualize the things you're grateful for, one by one, and let the feeling of gratitude fill your heart. If your mind starts to wander, gently guide it back to your breath and your blessings. Practicing gratitude meditation can help you connect with your inner self and foster a deeper appreciation for the world around you.

Now, don't forget to express your gratitude to others. Reach out to your loved ones, tell them how much they mean to you, and watch your relationships flourish. A simple "thank you" can go a long way in making someone's day brighter. As Black women, it's essential to uplift and support one another. So, make it a habit to acknowledge and appreciate the people who bring joy, love, and laughter to your life.

A great way to encourage self-reflection and introspection is to ask yourself, "What am I grateful for today *that I might have overlooked*?" Sometimes, it's easy to take the little things for granted, but when we pause and truly consider our blessings, we unlock a whole new level of gratitude. This, in turn, promotes personal growth and self-awareness.

Alright, we've covered creating a gratitude practice, and I'm sure you're feeling inspired to embrace thankfulness in your daily life.

But the magic doesn't stop there. Next, we are going to discuss how gratitude can open the door to even more blessings and opportunities.

When we practice gratitude, we create a positive energy that attracts abundance in all aspects of our lives. You know that saying, "like attracts like?" Well, that's precisely what we're doing here. By focusing on the good, we invite more good into our lives. It's like an abundance magnet!

## ATTRACTING ABUNDANCE THROUGH THANKFULNESS

Alright, now that we've explored creating a gratitude practice, let's dive into how thankfulness can help you attract abundance in your life. You see, when we actively express gratitude, we're not just feeling good and elevating our mood; we're also opening ourselves up to receive more blessings. Remember, what we focus on expands, and if we focus on the positive, we can manifest even more positive experiences.

Think of gratitude as a magnet for abundance. When we're thankful for what we have, we're sending out positive vibes to the universe, and in return, the universe responds with more blessings. So, how can you, my beautiful and powerful sister, harness this power to attract abundance in your life?

First, let's talk about being intentional with your gratitude. It's not enough to just say "thank you" and move on. Take a moment to genuinely feel gratitude for the blessings in your life. Whether it's your loving family, your beautiful home, or your steady job, feel the warmth and love that gratitude brings. Trust me, when you truly feel it in your heart, the universe will take notice.

Next, let's discuss affirmations. Affirmations are a powerful way to reprogram your mind to focus on the positive. Try incorporating gratitude-based affirmations into your daily routine.

For example, say to yourself, "I am grateful for the abundance flowing into my life," or "I am thankful for the love and support of my friends and family." Repeat these affirmations daily and watch as your mindset shifts, and abundance flows your way.

Now, here's a little challenge for you: keep a gratitude and abundance journal. In this journal, not only will you jot down the things you're grateful for, but you'll also write down the abundance you wish to attract. Be specific and write in the present tense, as if you've already received it. This practice helps you focus on what you want, and it sends a clear message to the universe about the blessings you're ready to receive.

Lastly, practice generosity. When we give from a place of gratitude and love, we create a ripple of positivity that can only come back to us. Whether it's donating to a cause close to your heart or simply lending a listening ear to a friend in need, being generous and kind can help you attract even more abundance into your life.

Are you ready to level up and let gratitude be your guide to abundance? Reflect on the following questions:

- In what areas of your life do you wish to attract more abundance?
- How can you be more intentional with your gratitude practice?
- What are some gratitude-based affirmations you can use to shift your mindset?
- How can you practice generosity in your daily life?

Remember, gratitude is a powerful force that can transform your life, and when you embrace thankfulness, you're opening yourself up to even more blessings and abundance.

## SUMMARY, ACTION STEPS & EXERCISES

- **Start a daily gratitude journal:** Each day, take a few minutes to write down at least three things you're grateful for. This simple practice will help you focus on the positive aspects of your life and cultivate a grateful mindset.
- **Use gratitude affirmations:** Create a set of positive, gratitude-based affirmations that resonate with you. Repeat them daily, either aloud or in your mind, to shift your mindset and reinforce the power of thankfulness.
- **Give back:** Find ways to be generous and show kindness to others. Whether it's through volunteering, donating, or simply being there for a friend, giving back creates a ripple of positivity that will attract even more abundance into your life.

---

We've made incredible progress on this self-care journey, and gratitude has been a game-changer. In this chapter, we unlocked the life-altering power of gratitude for our mental well-being and how it opens the door to a positive mindset. Remember, cherishing both big and small blessings helps us cultivate optimism and emotional balance.

Having harnessed gratitude's power, let's keep the self-care and personal growth momentum going. Next up, we'll dive into mindfulness, learning how to be present and aware in our daily lives. This newfound presence will bring even more peace, balance, and joy. Let's master mindfulness together and build a life overflowing with peace, love, and abundance.

Hey girl,

I hope the book is aiding your self-empowerment journey. If so, please consider leaving a review.

Your feedback not only lets me know what resonates with you, but also helps more Black women discover the book and its transformative message.

<u>LEAVE A QUICK REVIEW</u>

US    SCAN ME    UK

Your support plays a significant role in promoting self-love and empowerment for Black women globally. Let's continue sharing the love!

With gratitude,

Jada Amari

# CHAPTER 4
# MINDFULNESS MAGIC

*"Mindfulness is simply being aware of what is happening right now without wishing it were different; enjoying the pleasant without holding on when it changes (which it will); being with the unpleasant without fearing it will always be this way (which it won't)." – James Baraz*

You know that feeling when you're running on autopilot, going through the motions of your day without really being present in the moment? It's like you're a spectator in your own life, rather than an active participant. You may find yourself constantly worrying about the future or ruminating on the past, feeling like you're missing out on the simple pleasures of the present.

Well, what if I told you that there's a simple practice that can help you break free from this cycle and cultivate a deeper sense of presence and awareness? It's called mindfulness, and it's a powerful tool for self-care and personal growth.

In this chapter, we'll explore the benefits of mindfulness, and include practical techniques to incorporate it into your daily routine. We'll also discuss common obstacles that may arise during your mindfulness journey and give you strategies to overcome them. Get ready to experience the magic of mindfulness and unlock your inner power.

Let's hop into the wonderful world of mindfulness and discover how it can bring more peace, clarity, and joy into your life.

## THE BENEFITS OF MINDFULNESS FOR SELF-CARE

Have you ever found yourself feeling overwhelmed and stressed out by the demands of daily life? As a Black woman, you may be juggling work, family, social obligations, and other responsibilities, which can take a toll on your mental and emotional well-being. That's where mindfulness comes in - it's a powerful tool that can help you manage stress and improve your overall quality of life.

At its core, mindfulness is about being fully present and aware in the present moment, without judgment or distraction. It involves paying attention to your thoughts, feelings, and sensations in a non-judgmental way, which can help you develop greater self-awareness and emotional regulation.

One of the key benefits of mindfulness for self-care is that it can help you manage stress and anxiety. When you're feeling overwhelmed or anxious, it's easy to get caught up in negative thoughts and emotions, which can make your stress levels even worse. By practicing mindfulness, you can learn to observe your thoughts and emotions without getting caught up in them, which can help you feel calmer and centered.

In addition to reducing stress, mindfulness can also improve your overall emotional and mental health. It can help you become more self-aware and develop a greater sense of acceptance and self-compassion. By practicing mindfulness, you can learn to observe your thoughts and emotions without judgment, which can help you manage anxiety, depression, and other mental health issues.

Mindfulness can also improve your physical health by lowering blood pressure, improving sleep quality, and reducing chronic pain. It can also enhance your cognitive function, including attention, memory, and decision-making.

To reap the benefits of mindfulness, it's essential to practice it regularly. There are many ways to incorporate mindfulness into your daily routine, such as through meditation, mindful breathing exercises, or body scans. The key is to find a technique that works for you and stick with it.

It's also important to note that mindfulness is not a quick fix or a one-time solution. It's a practice that requires commitment and patience. You may encounter obstacles, such as racing thoughts or distractions, but with practice, you can overcome these challenges and cultivate a deeper sense of presence and awareness.

Incorporating mindfulness into your daily self-care routine can have a profound impact on your well-being. By cultivating greater self-awareness and emotional regulation, you can improve your ability to manage stress and enjoy life to the fullest. So take some time to explore the benefits of mindfulness and see how it can help you unlock your inner power and embrace abundance with unstoppable confidence.

## TECHNIQUES TO PRACTICE MINDFULNESS DAILY

Now that we've talked about the benefits of mindfulness for self-care, let's get into some practical techniques you can use to practice mindfulness daily.

Mindfulness is all about cultivating awareness of the present moment and accepting things as they are without judgment. It can help you reduce stress, anxiety, and negative thinking patterns, while improving your overall well-being. And the good news is, it doesn't require any fancy equipment or a lot of time.

One of the easiest ways to practice mindfulness is through breathing exercises. Find a quiet place where you won't be disturbed, sit comfortably with your back straight, and focus your attention on your breath. Take slow, deep breaths, feeling the air fill your lungs and exhaling slowly. Notice the sensation of your breath in your body and let go of any thoughts that may arise. If your mind wanders, gently bring your attention back to your breath. Do this for a few minutes every day, and you'll start to feel calmer and more centered.

Another way to practice mindfulness is through body scanning. Lie down or sit comfortably, and slowly bring your attention to each part of your body, starting from your toes and moving up to your head. Notice any sensations you feel without judging them as good or bad. If you notice any tension or discomfort, breathe into that area, and exhale slowly to release the tension. This exercise can help you become more aware of your body and release any physical tension you may be holding.

You can also practice mindfulness while doing everyday activities, like washing dishes or taking a shower. Pay attention to the sensory experience of the activity - the feel of the water, the smell of the soap, the sound of the water running. By bringing your full attention to the present moment, you can turn mundane tasks into opportunities for mindfulness.

Finally, a gratitude practice can also be a form of mindfulness. Take a few minutes every day to reflect on things you're grateful for - big or small. Notice the positive emotions that come up as you think about them and allow yourself to fully appreciate them. This practice can help shift your focus from what's going wrong to what's going right in your life.

Remember, mindfulness is a practice - it's not about doing it perfectly, but about showing up and making the effort every day. Start with just a few minutes a day and gradually build up your practice as you feel comfortable. And don't beat yourself up if you miss a day or don't feel like you're making progress - just keep showing up and practicing self-compassion.

I hope these techniques help you incorporate mindfulness into your daily routine and improve your overall well-being. Keep in mind that everyone's mindfulness journey is unique, so be patient and compassionate with yourself as you explore what works best for you.

## OVERCOMING OBSTACLES IN YOUR MINDFULNESS JOURNEY

Hey, now that we've covered techniques to practice mindfulness daily, let's talk about the challenges you might face on your mindfulness journey. It's important to remember that no matter how long you've been practicing mindfulness, everyone struggles at some point. The key is to be kind to yourself and keep pushing through those challenges.

One of the biggest obstacles you might face is finding time for mindfulness in your busy life. As a black woman, you likely have many responsibilities and obligations, whether it's work, family, or community involvement. It can be hard to find even a few minutes to sit down and practice mindfulness.

But here's the thing: mindfulness doesn't have to take a lot of time. Even a few minutes a day can make a big difference in your mental health and well-being. So, instead of trying to find an hour to meditate every day, try starting with just five minutes. Wake up a little earlier, or take a break during your workday, and use that time to focus on your breath and be present in the moment. As you get more comfortable with your mindfulness practice, you can gradually increase the time.

Another obstacle you might face is staying motivated to practice mindfulness. Sometimes it can feel like just another thing on your to-do list, and it's easy to fall out of the habit. When that happens, remember why you started practicing mindfulness in the first place. Maybe you wanted to reduce stress, or improve your sleep, or be more present with your loved ones. Whatever your reasons, keep them in mind and let them motivate you to keep going.

You can also try mixing up your mindfulness practice to keep it fresh and interesting. Maybe one day you meditate, and the next day you go for a mindful walk in nature. Or maybe you try a new mindfulness app or read a book on mindfulness to keep learning and growing.

Finally, another common obstacle to mindfulness is dealing with distractions and racing thoughts. When you sit down to practice mindfulness, your mind might start racing with thoughts about your day, your to-do list, or your worries. When that happens, don't beat yourself up or get discouraged. Instead, acknowledge the thoughts and gently bring your attention back to your breath or your body. It might take some practice, but over time you'll get better at letting go of those distractions and staying present in the moment.

So there you have it! No matter what obstacles you might face on your mindfulness journey, remember to be kind to yourself, stay motivated, mix things up, and let go of distractions. With a little patience and persistence, you'll be well on your way to a more mindful, peaceful, and empowered life.

## SUMMARY, ACTION STEPS & EXERCISES

- Schedule time for mindfulness practice every day. Start small, with just a few minutes each day, and gradually increase the time as you become more comfortable. Remember, consistency is key when it comes to developing any new habit, including mindfulness.
- Use mindfulness techniques in your daily life. Practice being fully present in the moment, focusing on your senses and the task at hand. Take deep breaths when you feel stressed, and take breaks throughout the day to simply be present and check in with yourself.
- Be gentle with yourself and remember that mindfulness is a journey. You will encounter obstacles along the way, but it's important to approach them with a sense of curiosity and self-compassion. When you find yourself struggling, take a step back, observe your thoughts and feelings, and use your mindfulness practice to help you move forward.

We've just wrapped up an amazing chapter about the basics of mindfulness and how it can transform your life. Now, it's time to put them into action. Remember, cultivating mindfulness is a journey, not a destination. Be patient with yourself and commit to integrating mindfulness practices into your daily routine. The more you practice, the easier it will become, and the more profound the benefits will be.

Are you ready for the next step in your self-care journey? Don't miss out on the next chapter, where we'll dive into the power of intention and how it can help you create a life that feels authentic and fulfilling. Get ready to ignite your intentions and unlock your true potential!

# CHAPTER 5
# ALIGNING YOUR ACTIONS WITH YOUR PURPOSE

"IF YOU DON'T KNOW WHERE YOU'RE GOING, ANY ROAD WILL TAKE YOU THERE." - ALICE WALKER

I t's time to ignite your intentions and align your actions with your deepest desires.

In this exciting chapter, we'll explore the concept of intention and why it plays such a vital role in our self-care journey. You'll learn how to set meaningful goals that truly resonate with your soul and discover practical strategies for turning those dreams into reality. We'll also discuss how to overcome obstacles and maintain focus on your path so you can fully embrace the abundant, fulfilling life you deserve.

Get ready to step into your power and start living your life with purpose, passion, and unstoppable confidence.

## THE IMPORTANCE OF INTENTION IN SELF-CARE

When it comes to living a fulfilling life, intention is the key. Think of it as the driving force that helps you navigate the complex journey of self-care, personal growth, and self-discovery. Setting clear intentions allows you to stay true to your desires and values, ensuring that your actions are in harmony with your deepest needs.

Now, let's explore why intention is such an essential ingredient in your self-care journey. For starters, intention helps you stay mindful and present in your daily life. When you have a clear understanding of your intentions, you can make conscious choices that align with your priorities. This way, you avoid getting caught up in the hustle and bustle of life, and instead, stay focused on what truly matters to you.

Moreover, intention fosters a sense of purpose and direction. When you set intentions for your self-care practice, you create a roadmap that leads you closer to your goals and aspirations. This not only helps you stay on track, but it also keeps you motivated and committed to your self-care journey.

So, how can you set intentions that truly resonate with your innermost desires? Start by taking some time for self-reflection. Ask yourself what you want to achieve in your self-care practice and how you want to feel as a result. Consider your values, priorities, and the areas in your life that need some extra love and attention.

Once you have a clear understanding of your intentions, write them down and keep them in a visible place. This could be on your bathroom mirror, in your planner, or even on your phone's wallpaper. By doing so, you'll have a daily reminder of your intentions, which can help you stay focused and motivated to pursue them.

It's also essential to revisit your intentions regularly, making adjustments when necessary. As you evolve and grow, your intentions might change as well. Embrace this flexibility and remember that your self-care journey is a dynamic process that requires adaptation and openness to change.

Intention is a powerful tool that can help you align your actions with your deepest desires and values. By setting clear intentions for your self-care practice, you can create a purposeful and fulfilling life that reflects your unique journey.

# TRANSFORMING DREAMS INTO REALITY

Now that we've explored the importance of intention in self-care, it's time to take the next step and transform those dreams into reality. As Black women, all we need to achieve our goals is the right mindset and tools, and we can overcome any obstacle and make our dreams a reality.

**Embracing the Growth Mindset**

Let's dive into the power of cultivating a growth mindset. I remember a time when I was trying to learn a new skill, and I kept hitting a wall. It was frustrating, and I felt like giving up. But then I realized that this was an opportunity for growth and learning. By embracing challenges and setbacks as stepping stones, we can persevere through difficulties and stay committed to our dreams, no matter the obstacles.

Take a moment to reflect on your own experiences. Have you ever faced a challenge that initially seemed insurmountable? Consider how reframing negative thoughts and self-talk can make a difference. Instead of dwelling on what you can't do or haven't accomplished, focus on the progress you've made and the lessons you've learned along the way. You're a work in progress, and every experience contributes to your growth and development.

**Surrounding Yourself with Positive Influences**

Now, let's discuss the impact of positive influences in our lives. Think about the people and resources that inspire and motivate you. For me, one of the most influential people in my life was my high school English teacher. She encouraged me to pursue my passion for writing, and her unwavering support helped shape the person I am today.

Surround yourself with friends, family members, mentors, or even books and podcasts that uplift and encourage you. This support network can make it easier to stay focused on your dreams and maintain the momentum necessary to achieve them.

## Taking Consistent Action Towards Your Dreams

When it comes to transforming dreams into reality, consistent action is crucial. Simply dreaming big and setting intentions isn't enough; you must also take steps, no matter how small, towards making those dreams a reality. I once set a goal to write a book, and it seemed like a daunting task. But by breaking it down into smaller tasks, like writing just one page a day, I was able to make steady progress and eventually complete the project.

Remember to celebrate your accomplishments along the way and use that sense of achievement to propel you forward. Every step counts, and each small victory brings you closer to realizing your dreams.

## Building Resilience for the Journey

Lastly, let's talk about resilience. Life is full of twists and turns, and setbacks and challenges can make us question our abilities or even want to give up. I've faced my share of obstacles, but I've learned that practicing self-compassion and reminding myself of my strength and determination is crucial for overcoming these hurdles.

Transforming dreams into reality involves embracing a growth mindset, surrounding yourself with positive influences, taking consistent action, and building resilience. With determination, persistence, and the right approach, you can create a life of abundance and fulfillment that aligns with your deepest desires.

## HOW TO SET AND PURSUE SOUL-ALIGNED GOALS

As a Black woman, you may often feel pressure to meet the expectations of others, whether it's your family, friends, or society. But it's important to remember that your life is yours to live, and your goals should reflect your unique desires and passions.

When setting goals, it's important to first identify your values and what's truly important to you. Take some time to reflect on what brings you joy, fulfillment, and a sense of purpose. Once you have a clear idea of what you want, you can set goals that align with your values and passions.

One helpful strategy is to use the SMART framework to set specific, measurable, achievable, relevant, and time-bound goals. For example, instead of setting a vague goal like "get healthier," you could set a SMART goal like "run a 5k race in three months." This goal is specific (run a 5k), measurable (you can track your progress and completion), achievable (it's realistic to train for a 5k in three months), relevant (it aligns with your desire to get healthier), and time-bound (you have a clear deadline of three months).

Another important factor to consider when setting goals is to make sure they're in alignment with your soul's purpose. Your soul's purpose is the reason you were put on this earth, and it's unique to you. To identify your soul's purpose, reflect on what you're passionate about, what brings you joy, and what you're naturally good at. Then, think about how you can use those passions and skills to make a positive impact in the world.

When pursuing your soul-aligned goals, it's important to stay focused and dedicated. This can be challenging, especially when life gets in the way. But remember, setbacks and obstacles are a natural part of the journey. When you face challenges, don't give up. Instead, recommit to your goals and take steps to overcome the obstacles in your path.

To stay motivated and inspired, surround yourself with positive influences. This could be a supportive community of like-minded individuals, motivational books or podcasts, or a mentor who can provide guidance and support. It's also important to celebrate your successes along the way, no matter how small. Recognize the progress you've made and use that momentum to keep pushing forward.

Setting and pursuing soul-aligned goals is essential to living a fulfilling life. By identifying your values, using the SMART framework, aligning with your soul's purpose, staying focused, and surrounding yourself with positive influences, you can achieve your goals and transform your dreams into reality.

## SUMMARY, ACTION STEPS & EXERCISES

- Write down your dreams and goals, and then break them down into smaller, achievable steps. By creating a roadmap to your desired destination, you can set yourself up for success and make your aspirations feel more tangible and attainable.
- Create a self-care routine that supports your mental, emotional, and spiritual well-being. Prioritize activities that help you feel grounded, centered, and aligned with your purpose. Whether it's practicing yoga, meditating, or journaling, make sure you're taking intentional steps to care of yourself.
- Surround yourself with positivity and support. Seek out mentors, friends, and family members who will uplift

and encourage you on your journey. Cultivate a community of like-minded individuals who share your values and will hold you accountable to your goals. Remember, you don't have to go at it alone – having a strong support system can make all the difference

---

In this chapter, we've journeyed through the compelling force of intention in self-care, discovering how it elevates mindfulness and purpose in your everyday life. We've also emphasized the significance of pursuing soul-aligned goals and shared tactics to turn your aspirations into reality. By converting intentions into concrete actions, you'll ignite meaningful change and unleash your inner power.

As we progress, it's time to delve into the rejuvenating practice of yoga. In our next chapter, we'll uncover how yoga nurtures physical and emotional well-being, alleviates stress, and fosters relaxation. Additionally, we'll explore the diverse types of yoga and guide you in choosing the style that resonates with your unique needs.

Believe in yourself, girl! With intention, dedication, and a sprinkle of self-care magic, you can tap into your power and embrace abundance with unwavering confidence.

# CHAPTER 6

# THE TRANSFORMATIVE ART OF YOGA

"YOGA IS NOT ABOUT TOUCHING YOUR TOES. IT'S ABOUT WHAT YOU LEARN ON THE WAY DOWN." - JIGAR GOR

Ever felt the weight of the world on your shoulders, leaving you longing for something to help you slow down, relax, and reconnect with your inner self? Well, get excited, because I've got some good news for you! Yoga might just be the answer you've been seeking.

In this chapter, we'll dive into the spiritual dimensions of yoga and uncover how it can benefit not only your physical health but also your mental and emotional well-being. Together, we'll explore the different types of yoga practices available to find the one that aligns with your unique needs and aspirations. Plus, we'll chat about how you can effortlessly incorporate yoga into your busy self-care routine, no matter how packed your schedule may be.

By the time you finish soaking up the wisdom in this chapter, you'll be equipped with all the knowledge and tools necessary to embark on your own transformative yoga journey. So, take a deep, calming breath, and prepare to unveil a practice that can help you find balance and inner peace amid life's storms. Embrace the journey, and get ready to discover the serenity that's been waiting for you all along.

## EXPLORING THE SPIRITUAL DIMENSIONS OF YOGA

Have you ever wondered why yoga has taken the world by storm? It's not just because it helps you get a toned body; it's also because it offers powerful spiritual benefits that can transform our lives. Let's explore the spiritual dimensions of yoga and how they can help Black women like us in our daily lives.

Yoga is not just a physical practice; it's a spiritual journey that connects our body, mind, and soul. When we step onto the mat, we're not only working on our flexibility and strength but also our inner resilience and wisdom. It's like our very own superpower, helping us tap into our divine feminine energy and unlock our true potential.

One of the many spiritual benefits of yoga is its ability to promote mindfulness and self-awareness. As we flow through the poses, we're encouraged to be present in the moment, to listen to our bodies, and to connect with our breath. This heightened sense of awareness allows us to better understand our emotions, thoughts, and desires, empowering us to make decisions that align with our true selves.

Now, let me share a little story about my friend Liana, a fellow sister who discovered the transformative power of yoga and mindfulness in her own life.

Liana was a successful marketing executive with a fast-paced, high-stress career. Despite her outward achievements, she found herself feeling overwhelmed and disconnected from her true passions. Seeking a way to manage her stress and find balance, Liana decided to give yoga a try.

As Liana began to incorporate yoga into her daily routine, she noticed a profound shift in her mindset. She found herself becoming more mindful and present, both on and off the mat. This newfound self-awareness allowed her to recognize the misalignment between her current career and her deepest desires.

Inspired by this inner transformation, Liana made the brave decision to leave her high-paying job in pursuit of a career that aligned with her passions and values. She enrolled in a yoga teacher training program and, after months of hard work and dedication, opened her own yoga studio focused on empowering and uplifting Black women.

Through her yoga practice, Liana not only discovered a powerful tool for stress relief but also unlocked her inner wisdom and intuition. Today, she's living a life that truly reflects her authentic self, and she's inspiring other Black women to do the same.

### Yoga's Spiritual Dimensions

Now, I know what you're thinking. How do you even begin to incorporate the spiritual dimensions of yoga into your life? Fear not, I've got you covered! Start by setting an intention before each practice. This can be a word, a phrase, or an affirmation that resonates with you and helps guide your practice. For example, you can set the intention to cultivate self-love, inner peace, or resilience. By doing this, you're not only working on your physical well-being but also nourishing your spirit and nurturing your personal growth.

Another way to deepen your spiritual connection during yoga is through meditation. Many yoga classes incorporate meditation at the beginning or end of the practice to help center the mind and connect with the breath. If you're new to meditation, don't worry, sis. It's all about finding a comfortable position, focusing on your breath, and letting your thoughts come and go without judgment. With time and practice, you'll find that meditation can be a powerful tool for self-reflection and introspection, helping you gain insight and clarity about your life.

Now that we've explored the spiritual dimensions of yoga, it's time to find the right practice for you. There are many styles and forms of yoga, each with its unique benefits and focus. From gentle Hatha yoga to the more challenging Ashtanga, there's something for everyone, regardless of your experience or fitness level.

## CHOOSING THE RIGHT YOGA PRACTICE FOR YOU

Having covered the spiritual dimensions of yoga, let's move on to finding the right yoga practice for you. It's crucial to choose a style that resonates with your unique needs, goals, and personality. Remember, your yoga journey is all about you!

As we dive into finding the right yoga practice for you, it's essential to remember that your yoga journey is all about your unique needs, goals, and personality. Let's explore a variety of practices in more depth, highlighting their unique focus and benefits, to help you make an informed choice.

### Hatha Yoga: Building a Strong Foundation

Hatha yoga is a gentle, slow-paced practice that's perfect for beginners and anyone seeking relaxation and stress relief. This style focuses on the fundamentals, including breathwork, balance, and alignment. Practicing Hatha yoga allows you to build a strong foundation, making it an ideal starting point for those new to yoga or looking to deepen their understanding of essential yoga postures.

## Vinyasa Yoga: Flowing with Grace

Vinyasa yoga, on the other hand, is more dynamic and focuses on synchronizing breath with movement. This practice creates a seamless flow of postures that build strength, flexibility, and stamina. If you're looking for a more vigorous workout that also fosters a sense of inner calm, Vinyasa might be the perfect choice.

## Ashtanga Yoga: Embracing Discipline and Structure

Ashtanga yoga is a more structured and intense practice that challenges you both physically and mentally. This style involves a series of set postures performed in a specific order, with a strong emphasis on breath and movement synchronization. If you're seeking a disciplined and challenging practice that encourages mental focus and self-growth, Ashtanga might be the right fit.

## Power Yoga: Building Strength and Confidence

Power yoga, as the name suggests, is a powerful and energetic practice designed to build strength, stamina, and flexibility. This style often incorporates challenging postures and sequences, making it a great choice if you're looking to push your limits and gain physical confidence.

## Yin Yoga: Releasing Deep Tension

Yin yoga is all about deep stretches and relaxation. This practice involves holding postures for extended periods, allowing you to target the connective tissues in your body and release deep-seated tension. If you're seeking a slower-paced practice that promotes relaxation, stress relief, and deep healing, Yin yoga might be the ideal choice.

So, how do you choose the right yoga practice for you?

Start by reflecting on your goals and preferences. Are you looking to improve flexibility, build strength, or find inner peace? What about the pace and intensity of the practice? Do you prefer a gentle, slow flow or a more vigorous, challenging workout? Yoga can be a powerful tool to help us navigate stress, build resilience, and cultivate self-love in a world that often tests our strength and spirit. So, consider how each yoga style might address your specific needs and experiences.

Once you have a clear idea of your preferences and goals, it's time to explore different yoga classes and teachers. Try out various styles and studios (or online classes) to see which resonates with you. Don't be afraid to step out of your comfort zone and try something new! Keep in mind that finding the right yoga practice can be a process of trial and error, so be patient with yourself and enjoy the journey.

Now, let's talk about how to make your chosen yoga practice work for you. It's essential to create a consistent routine that fits your schedule and lifestyle. Whether you prefer early morning sessions to start your day on a positive note or evening classes to unwind and relax, find a time that works best for you and commit to it. Consistency is key!

And don't forget to personalize your practice. It's essential to remember that each person's experience is unique. One of the keys to a successful and safe practice is to ensure you're maintaining the correct pose and making modifications based on your own abilities. Remember, failing to perform the poses correctly can lead to injury, so it's crucial to pay attention to your body's signals.

Always prioritize personalizing your practice to meet your body's needs and your comfort level. Don't hesitate to modify poses and sequences to suit you. Remember, yoga is not about keeping up with the person on the mat next to you. It's about connecting with your inner self and nurturing your mind, body, and soul.

As you flow through your practice, make a conscious effort to listen to your body, honor your limits, and celebrate your progress. Recognize that each day on the mat is an opportunity for growth and self-discovery, and by tuning into your own needs, you'll cultivate a yoga practice that's both empowering and sustainable.

As you continue to explore different yoga styles and practices, take some time to reflect on your journey. Ask yourself questions like,

"What have I learned about myself through my yoga practice?"

"How has yoga helped me grow and evolve?"

These reflections can provide valuable insights into your personal growth, self-awareness, and overall well-being. Embrace this process, and remember that your yoga practice is a powerful tool for self-discovery, empowerment, and transformation.

As we've gone over which type of yoga is the best for you, it's time to incorporate yoga into your self-care routine.

## INCORPORATING YOGA INTO YOUR SELF-CARE ROUTINE

Now that we've talked about choosing the right yoga practice for you, let's dive into incorporating yoga into your self-care routine. I know, it might seem like a daunting task, but trust me, it's easier than you think. Let me guide you through the process with some simple steps that will make yoga an essential part of your life.

First things first, let's talk about creating a dedicated space for your yoga practice. Having a special place in your home can help you stay consistent and focused. Find a spot that's comfortable, quiet, and free from distractions. Add some personal touches like candles, inspiring quotes, or even a vision board to make it feel like your sanctuary. Remember, this is your space to unwind, connect with yourself, and grow.

Next, let's set some realistic goals for your yoga practice. Start small, maybe commit to practicing 10-15 minutes a day, and gradually increase the duration as you become more comfortable. Don't forget to celebrate your progress and milestones, whether it's mastering a challenging pose or noticing improvements in your mental well-being.

Consistency is key, but so is flexibility. Life happens, and sometimes, you might miss a session or feel like you need to switch up your routine. That's totally fine, girl! Listen to your body and adapt your practice as needed. The goal is to make yoga a sustainable and enjoyable part of your self-care journey.

Now, let's talk about staying motivated and accountable. Share your yoga journey with friends and family, or even join a supportive online community. Surrounding yourself with like-minded individuals can help keep you inspired, motivated, and accountable. Plus, it's always fun to exchange stories, tips, and encouragement with others.

Speaking of encouragement, remind yourself of the reasons why you started practicing yoga in the first place. Is it to improve your mental health, increase flexibility, or simply to have some "me-time"? Keep these reasons in mind as you practice and use them as motivation to stay committed.

And finally, have fun with your practice, sis! Yoga is not just about the physical postures but also about self-discovery, personal growth, and connecting with your inner self. Embrace the journey, learn from your experiences, and allow yourself to be playful and curious. Remember, you're doing this for you, so enjoy the process.

Take a moment to reflect on your yoga journey so far. What challenges have you faced, and how have you overcome them? How has your practice evolved over time, and what have you learned about yourself? Self-reflection is a powerful tool for personal growth and self-awareness, so don't be afraid to dig deep and uncover your inner wisdom.

Incorporating yoga into your self-care routine can be a transformative experience that brings about growth, empowerment, and self-love. Explore different yoga styles and find the one that resonates with you and your needs. By creating a dedicated space, setting realistic goals, staying motivated, and embracing the journey, you're well on your way to making yoga an essential part of your life. Keep shining, and remember: the power to unlock your potential and reclaim your life lies within you. Namaste!

## SUMMARY, ACTION STEPS & EXERCISES

- Set an intention for your yoga practice, focusing on the spiritual dimensions you'd like to explore, such as self-awareness, inner peace, or self-love.
- Research various yoga styles and choose one that resonates with your goals, personal preferences, and lifestyle, giving you the foundation to grow and evolve in your practice.
- Schedule a consistent time for yoga in your daily or weekly routine, and create a dedicated, comfortable space in your home to nurture your practice and support your self-care journey.

Now, you've delved into the transformative art of yoga and discovered the spiritual dimensions of this ancient practice. Yoga is not just a physical exercise, but also a spiritual practice that can help you connect with something greater than yourself. By exploring the different types of yoga practices, you can find one that fits your unique needs and goals. Incorporating yoga into your self-care routine can enhance your overall well-being and reduce stress.

As you continue on your journey of self-care and personal growth, remember to be patient with yourself. Yoga is a practice, and it takes time and dedication to see the benefits. With consistent practice and a positive attitude, you can cultivate a deep connection with your mind, body, and soul.

Next up, we will explore the power of journaling and how it can help you unlock your inner wisdom. Journaling is a powerful tool for self-reflection and personal growth. By putting your thoughts and feelings down on paper, you can gain clarity and insight into your life. Get ready to discover a powerful tool for self-reflection and personal growth.

# CHAPTER 7
# JOURNALING YOUR JOURNEY: UNLOCKING INNER WISDOM

*"Write it down, girl, so your heart can read it, your mind can feel it, and your soul can breathe it." - Maya Angelou*

Did you know, that the simple act of putting pen to paper has the power to transform your life? That's right, journaling is an incredible tool that can help you tap into your inner wisdom and unlock the secrets of your soul. In this chapter, we'll delve into the amazing benefits of journaling for your spiritual self-care journey and share insightful tips to create a successful journaling practice. We'll also provide thought-provoking prompts that'll guide you through deep self-reflection.

As we journey through this eye-opening chapter, you'll discover the numerous advantages of journaling, such as heightened self-awareness, reduced stress, and enhanced problem-solving abilities. We'll chat about various journaling techniques, ensuring you establish a practice that resonates with your unique needs and desires. Plus, you'll receive soul-stirring prompts designed to guide you through the process of self-reflection. These prompts will help you gain clarity, embrace growth, and ultimately, flourish on your spiritual self-care journey.

So get ready, to harness the transformative power of journaling, as we embark on this enlightening adventure together. Prepare to uncover your innermost thoughts and feelings, and watch how your life begins to change in ways you never thought possible.

## HOW JOURNALING SUPPORTS SPIRITUAL SELF-CARE

Journaling is an amazing self-care tool and is something you absolutely need in your life! Trust me, it can do wonders for your spiritual well-being, and I've seen firsthand how it helps unlock that inner wisdom of yours.

You know those moments when you're feeling overwhelmed or lost, and all you want to do is spill your heart out to your closest friend? Well, journaling is like having a heart-to-heart conversation with yourself, your very own inner bestie. It's a judgment-free zone where you can let your thoughts and emotions flow, and it's incredibly powerful for gaining clarity, insight, and self-awareness.

Let me share a little story about Aaliyah. Life was throwing her some serious curveballs, and she felt like she was stuck in a maze, unsure of which way to turn. She decided to give journaling a try, and every day she'd write about her thoughts, feelings, and experiences. Before she knew it, she started noticing patterns and recurring themes in her entries. This self-reflection helped her figure out her true passion – empowering others through mentorship. Journaling was the key that helped Aaliyah unlock her inner wisdom and find her purpose.

Journaling is an essential tool for spiritual self-care as it provides a space for you to truly connect with your inner self. By putting pen to paper, you give voice to your emotions, and it can be incredibly therapeutic. Plus, as you document your journey, you'll start to see your growth, and that's an amazing feeling, trust me.

Journaling also allows you to recognize and celebrate your accomplishments, no matter how big or small. It's easy to get caught up in our daily lives and forget to appreciate the progress we've made. But when you write it all down, you'll be reminded of your strength and resilience, boosting your self-confidence and self-love.

Remember, this is all about you and your journey, so make it personal and let your authentic self shine. Your spiritual self-care will thank you, and who knows, you might just find yourself feeling more connected, empowered, and inspired than ever before.

Ready to put some tips into practice and start journaling to unlock the best version of yourself?

## TIPS FOR A SUCCESSFUL JOURNALING PRACTICE

Girl, I've got your back! I know life can be hectic and finding the time and motivation to start journaling can be tough. But trust me, with these tips, you'll be writing like there's no tomorrow and loving every minute of it.

**Make It a Habit:** Consistency is key, sis! Set aside a specific time each day for your journaling practice. Maybe it's first thing in the morning, during your lunch break, or before bed. Choose a time that works best for you and stick to it. Remember, it takes about 21 days to form a habit, so be patient with yourself.

**Find Your Space:** Create a comfortable, inviting space to write in. It could be a cozy corner in your living room, your bedroom, or even your favorite coffee shop. Having a designated space helps you focus and sets the mood for some serious self-reflection.

**Choose Your Journal and Writing Tools:** Go shopping for a journal that speaks to your soul. It might be a fancy leather-bound notebook, a spiral notebook with your favorite quote on the cover, or even a digital journaling app. Pair it with a pen that feels good in your hand, and you're all set!

**Let It Flow:** When it comes to journaling, there's no right or wrong way to do it. Allow yourself to write freely without worrying about grammar or spelling. Release your thoughts and feelings onto the page, and don't hold back. You might be surprised at what comes up when you give yourself permission to be open and honest.

**Keep It Private:** Your journal is a sacred space for you to explore your inner world. Give yourself the freedom to express yourself without fear of judgment. This means keeping your journal private, unless you choose to share it with someone you trust. If you're worried about someone finding your journal, consider using a digital journaling app with password protection.

**Mix It Up:** Don't be afraid to get creative with your journaling practice. Try different formats, like writing in bullet points, creating mind maps, or even drawing pictures. Experiment with different journaling techniques, such as gratitude journaling, dream journaling, or freewriting. The more you mix it up, the more you'll discover what works best for you.

**Reflect and Grow:** Take time to reread your journal entries every now and then. You might notice patterns, themes, or recurring thoughts that can help you gain insight into your life. Reflect on your experiences and use that knowledge to grow and make positive changes.

Remember that journaling is a personal journey. It's about discovering your inner wisdom and giving yourself the gift of self-reflection. Start incorporating these tips into your journaling practice and watch as your spiritual self-care reaches new heights.

Up next, let's dive deep into self-reflection with some prompts to help you explore your thoughts, feelings, and beliefs. These prompts will inspire you to dig deeper and uncover the hidden gems within your soul.

## PROMPTS TO DIVE DEEP INTO SELF-REFLECTION

Having highlighted tips for a successful journaling practice, let's explore some thought-provoking prompts to help you dive deep into self-reflection. These prompts will guide you on your journey to self-discovery, empowerment, and growth, sis. Remember, there's no right or wrong way to respond to these prompts – the key is to be honest with yourself and let your thoughts flow. Grab your journal and jot these down!

- What are your core values, and how do they influence your daily life? Consider the principles that guide your decision-making and think about how they align with your actions.
- Reflect on a recent challenge you've faced. What did you learn from this experience, and how can you apply that lesson to future situations? It's time to turn those setbacks into comebacks, girl!
- Think about a time when you felt truly proud of yourself. What did you accomplish, and what strengths

did you exhibit? Embrace your inner power and let that confidence shine.

- What does self-love mean to you, and how do you practice it in your daily life? Remember, you are a queen, and you deserve all the love and care in the world.

- If you could give your younger self one piece of advice, what would it be? Reflect on the wisdom you've gained over the years, and think about how it could have impacted your past self.

- Envision your ideal life five years from now. What are you doing, and who are you surrounded by? Set your intentions, and start working towards that dream, sis!

- What are three things you're grateful for today? Cultivate an attitude of gratitude and watch as it transforms your mindset and your life.

- What are your top three goals for the next year? Break them down into actionable steps and start working towards making them a reality. You've got this, girl!

- Reflect on a time when someone's kindness made a difference in your life. How did it make you feel, and how can you pay that kindness forward?

- What does success mean to you, and how will you know when you've achieved it? Remember, success is a personal journey – define it for yourself, and don't let anyone else's expectations hold you back.

- What are the most significant sources of stress in your life, and how can you work to alleviate them? Reflect on the aspects of your life that weigh you down and brainstorm ways to create balance and harmony.

- If you could have a conversation with one person who has passed away, who would it be and why? Think about what you would discuss and the insights you might gain from this encounter.

- How do you define personal growth, and what steps are you taking to achieve it? Consider the areas in which you'd like to evolve and the actions you can take to make it happen.

- What brings you the most joy in life, and how can you incorporate more of that into your daily routine? Recognize the activities, people, and experiences that light you up and fuel your happiness.

- Reflect on a time when you stepped out of your comfort zone and took a risk. What did you learn from that experience, and how did it impact your personal growth? Embrace the lessons and celebrate your courage, girl!

- If you could travel anywhere in the world, where would you go and why? Visualize your dream destination and the experiences that await you there. What draws you to this place, and what adventures would you embark on?

- How would you describe your support system, and how do they contribute to your well-being? Consider the relationships that uplift and inspire you, and express gratitude for the love and encouragement they provide.

As you work through these prompts, remember that self-reflection is an ongoing process. It's not about having all the answers right away, but rather about exploring your thoughts, feelings, and beliefs to gain a deeper understanding of yourself. Be patient with yourself and give yourself the space to grow and evolve.

Don't be afraid to revisit these prompts over time, as your perspective and experiences may change. The key is to stay open and honest with yourself, and to trust the process. As you continue to journal your journey, you'll unlock the inner wisdom that will guide you towards personal growth, empowerment, and unstoppable confidence. Keep shining!

## SUMMARY, ACTION STEPS & EXERCISES

- Set aside 10-15 minutes each day for journaling: Commit to a daily practice and choose a specific time and place that feels comfortable and sacred to you. This consistency will help you develop a deeper connection with your inner wisdom.
- Choose a journaling method that resonates with you: Experiment with different styles of journaling, such as free writing, bullet journaling, or gratitude journaling. Find what works best for you and allows you to express yourself authentically.
- Use self-reflective prompts to explore your thoughts and emotions: Start your journaling sessions with thought-provoking questions or statements, such as "What am I grateful for today?" or "How can I show myself more love and compassion?" These prompts will encourage you to dive deep into your feelings and beliefs, supporting your spiritual self-care journey.

As we wrap up this chapter on journaling, let's take a moment to reflect on the gems we've collected along the way, sis. Throughout this enlightening journey, we've discovered how journaling can be an invaluable tool for self-discovery and spiritual growth. It's truly amazing how putting pen to paper can help us tap into our inner wisdom and elevate our self-awareness.

As you embark on this transformative path, remember that self-discovery is an ongoing process. Be patient with yourself, trust the journey, and know that you have everything you need within you to thrive.

Now that you've unlocked the power of journaling, it's time to take the next step towards self-empowerment. In the upcoming chapter, we'll dive into the world of affirmations and explore how embracing positive self-talk can help you reaffirm your worth and build unstoppable confidence. So, grab your pen, your favorite journal, and get ready to take your spiritual self-care to new heights!

# CHAPTER 8
## AFFIRM YOUR WORTH

*"Believe in your infinite potential. Your only limitations are those you set upon yourself." - Roy T. Bennett*

We all have those moments when we doubt ourselves or let negativity take the driver's seat. But don't worry, you're not alone. I've been there too! In fact, that's what inspired me to write this book. I wanted to share my experiences and discoveries with my fellow queens, so that we can all rise above the noise and embrace the fabulous beings we truly are.

In this chapter, we'll dive into the world of affirmations, exploring their transformative power and how they can help us connect with our inner goddess. Trust me, once you start using affirmations, you'll wonder how you ever lived without them!

But don't worry, I won't just throw you into the deep end. We'll start by breaking down the importance of positive self-talk and how to silence that pesky inner critic. I'll share some of my favorite affirmations that have carried me through tough times and helped me become the strong, empowered woman I am today.

And guess what? I'm going to help you craft your very own affirmations, tailored to your unique dreams and aspirations. You'll be feeling like the fierce, unstoppable queen you were always meant to be in no time!

So, are you ready to embark on this journey of self-discovery, growth, and empowerment? I know I am! Let's get our spiritual self-care on and unlock the universe's secrets to living our best lives. Together, we're about to create some serious magic.

## THE POWER OF AFFIRMATIONS IN SELF-CARE

Imagine this: our girl Lacresha has been struggling with her self-esteem lately. She's an amazing, hard-working Black woman, but sometimes the stress of life gets her down. One day, her best friend introduces her to the concept of affirmations. At first, Lacresha is skeptical, but she decides to give it a try. Each morning, she looks in the mirror and repeats affirmations like, "I am strong," "I am worthy," and "I am enough." Before she knows it, her confidence starts to soar, and she feels more empowered than ever.

This story isn't just about Lacresha – it's about you and countless other Black women who can benefit from the power of affirmations. When you repeat positive, empowering statements to yourself, you're rewiring your brain to focus on the good in your life. You're telling yourself that you're deserving of all the greatness the universe has to offer, and you are!

Affirmations have been proven to reduce stress, boost self-esteem, and improve overall mental well-being. They're like a pep talk from your best friend, a hug from your mama, and a high-five from your biggest cheerleader, all rolled into one.

When we talk about the power of affirmations, we're not just talking about some feel-good words. We're talking about real, tangible changes in the way you see yourself and the world around you. Affirmations help shift your mindset from negative self-talk to positive self-love. This shift in mindset can be life-changing, enabling you to face challenges head-on and to trust in your abilities.

As women of color, we consistently face individual trials during our day-to-day activities, and our mental and emotional well-being can take a hit. By incorporating affirmations into your self-care routine, you're taking a stand against those negative messages and reminding yourself that you are resilient, powerful, and deserving of all the goodness life has to offer.

So, how can you harness the power of affirmations in your self-care journey? Start by setting aside a few minutes each day to practice your affirmations. Whether it's first thing in the morning or during your evening wind-down, find a quiet space where you can focus on your thoughts and speak your truth. Repeat your affirmations with conviction and let the positive energy wash over you.

Remember, the journey to self-love and empowerment isn't always easy, but with the right tools in hand, like affirmations, you're well on your way to unlocking your full potential.

Now, it's time to get personal. Let's dive deeper into crafting personalized affirmations that work for you. By understanding the power of language and thought, you'll be able to create affirmations that resonate with you on a deep level, reinforcing your worth, and empowering you to achieve your dreams. So, let's get started on crafting personalized affirmations that will help you unleash your full potential!

## CRAFTING PERSONALIZED AFFIRMATIONS

Now that we've talked about the power of affirmations in self-care, let's dive deeper into crafting personalized affirmations that resonate with your unique experiences, sis. Remember, affirmations work best when they feel authentic and meaningful to you, so let's take the time to make sure they're tailored to your journey.

Before you start creating your affirmations, it's crucial to take a moment and reflect on your values, goals, and the areas in your life that might need a little extra love and encouragement. Are you working on building self-confidence? Strengthening your relationships? Or maybe manifesting career success? Identifying your focus areas will help you create affirmations that are powerful and purposeful.

When crafting your affirmations, be sure to use positive, present-tense language. For example, instead of saying, "I will be successful," say, "I am successful." This shift in language helps your mind accept the affirmation as a reality, right here and now. Besides, as a strong, vibrant, Black woman, you deserve to live in the present moment, honey!

As you work on your affirmations, make sure they are specific and actionable. While "I am confident" is a great start, take it a step further by saying, "I confidently speak my truth and express my needs." This specificity empowers you to take control of your life and manifest the changes you desire.

Let me tell you – when it comes to crafting your personalized affirmations, don't be afraid to get creative! Use language that resonates with you and your culture. If there's a particular song lyric, Bible verse, or wise words from a loved one that speaks to your soul, incorporate it into your affirmation. After all, embracing your roots and your community is a powerful way to feel connected and supported on this journey.

Now, let's talk about the importance of repetition. Just like any good skincare routine, the magic of affirmations lies in consistency. So, repeat your affirmations daily, even multiple times a day if you can. You'll be amazed at how quickly your thoughts and beliefs about yourself start to shift. Trust me, I've been there.

Speaking of which, I remember a time when I had doubts about my writing. I kept questioning whether my voice mattered and if I was making a difference. But, I started using affirmations like "I am a powerful and inspiring storyteller" and "My words uplift and empower those who read them," and before I knew it, not only did my confidence soar, but my writing improved too!

Once you've crafted your personalized affirmations, it's time to make them a part of your everyday routine. You can write them down and place them where you'll see them every day – think bathroom mirror, fridge door, or even on your phone as a reminder. Or you could set aside a few minutes each day to stand in front of the mirror, look yourself in the eyes, and say your affirmations out loud. Trust me, it may feel a bit awkward at first, but there's something powerful about speaking your truth and owning your worth.

So, take the time to craft your personalized affirmations and integrate them into your daily life. Remember that you're not just speaking words – you're actively creating the life you want and deserve. Embrace the journey and watch as you unlock your power, reclaim your life, and embrace abundance with unstoppable confidence.

## INTEGRATING AFFIRMATIONS INTO YOUR DAILY LIFE

Now that we've talked about crafting personalized affirmations, it's crucial to explore the ways you can seamlessly integrate these powerful tools into your daily life. Despite the chaos of our everyday routines, incorporating affirmations can be surprisingly simple and can make a significant impact on your overall well-being.

The first step to integrating affirmations into your daily life is to create a morning ritual. Just as breakfast nourishes your body, beginning your day with affirmations feeds your soul. By setting aside a few moments each morning to recite your affirmations out loud or write them in a journal, you lay the foundation for a day filled with positivity, self-love, and empowerment. This practice helps you start your day with intention and sets the stage for a more focused and self-aware mindset.

Visual reminders are another effective way to incorporate affirmations throughout your day. By placing your affirmations where you'll frequently encounter them, you create opportunities for consistent reinforcement of your positive self-talk. Consider posting your affirmations on your bathroom mirror, refrigerator, computer monitor, or even setting them as reminders on your phone. These visual cues serve as gentle reminders of your worth and help keep your mindset in check.

Another powerful approach to embedding affirmations into your daily life is through meditation or prayer. By incorporating your personalized affirmations into your spiritual practice, you strengthen the connection between your self-worth and your higher power, whatever that may be for you. This deepened connection fosters an environment in which you can embrace the full potential of your affirmations and cultivate a sense of inner peace.

A crucial aspect of integrating affirmations into your daily life is consistency. Just like any other habit, affirmations require repetition to be truly effective. Committing to daily practice allows these positive statements to become second nature and ensures that they have a lasting impact on your mindset.

As you strive to maintain consistency, it's essential to approach the process with patience and self-compassion. Remember, Rome wasn't built in a day! It takes time for new habits to take root, and you may encounter setbacks along the way. Be gentle with yourself during this journey, and don't be afraid to modify your affirmations or your approach as needed.

To further enhance the impact of your affirmations, consider pairing them with self-reflection and introspection. Take some time to journal or engage in quiet contemplation about your affirmations, examining how they relate to your life, beliefs, and values. This process can deepen your understanding of yourself and promote personal growth and self-awareness.

Lastly, don't forget to have some fun and get creative with your affirmations. Embrace your inner wordsmith and play with language, incorporating humor, wit, and phrases that resonate with your unique experience as a Black woman. This personal touch will make your affirmations more enjoyable, engaging, and memorable.

Integrating affirmations into your daily life can be a transformative experience, providing you with the tools to embrace positivity, self-love, and empowerment. By incorporating these practices into your routine and approaching the process with consistency, patience, and self-compassion, you can unlock your power, reclaim your life, and embrace abundance with unstoppable confidence.

## SUMMARY, ACTION STEPS & EXERCISES

- Identify and counteract negative self-talk: Pay attention to your thoughts and, whenever you catch yourself engaging in self-criticism or doubt, replace them with empowering, positive statements that remind you of your worth and abilities.
- Create personalized affirmations that resonate with you: Reflect on your values, goals, and strengths, and use them to craft powerful, meaningful affirmations that reinforce your self-belief and confidence.
- Incorporate affirmations into your daily routine: Set aside time each day to recite your affirmations, either silently or aloud. Try repeating them during your morning routine, while looking in the mirror, or during moments of quiet reflection throughout the day. This practice will help solidify positive self-talk as an integral part of your self-care journey.

We've come a long way on this journey, and I'm so proud of you for embracing the power of affirmations and positive self-talk. In this chapter, we've delved into the significance of affirmations in your self-care practice and how they can transform your mindset and elevate your spirit. And now, you're equipped to create personalized affirmations that resonate with your goals and dreams.

Remember, integrating affirmations into your daily life as a consistent practice helps you take control of your narrative and reclaim your power. Trust me, when you do this regularly, you'll feel the shift in your energy, confidence, and outlook on life.

So, what's next for our spiritual self-care adventure? In the upcoming chapter, we'll explore bonding with nature and finding your tribe. Nature has a remarkable way of healing and grounding us, allowing us to access our inner wisdom and rejuvenate our souls. And when it comes to finding your tribe, there's nothing more empowering than surrounding yourself with like-minded, supportive people who uplift and inspire you.

Let's immerse ourselves in nature's beauty and build a strong, supportive tribe together. We'll dive deeper into our spiritual self-care journey, unlocking even greater abundance and happiness in our lives. By connecting with the earth and our community, we can amplify our personal growth and empowerment even more.

Stay motivated, stay inspired, and most importantly, stay true to yourself. Remember, you're a force to be reckoned! Together, we'll uplift and support one another every step of the way. So, take a deep breath, and let's continue on this incredible journey of self-discovery and personal growth.

# CHAPTER 9
# CONNECTING WITH THE EARTH AND YOUR TRIBE

*"In nature, nothing is perfect and everything is perfect. Trees can be contorted, bent in weird ways, and they're still beautiful." - Alice Walker*

magine strolling through a serene garden, breathing in the sweet fragrance of flowers, or sitting by a calming waterfall, feeling the gentle mist on your face – these moments have a special kind of magic, don't they? This enchantment, my friend, comes from the harmonious connection between our spirit and the natural world. Mother Earth has always been our greatest teacher, healer, and nurturer, offering her wisdom and love to guide us on our path to self-discovery.

In this chapter, we'll delve deep into the wonders of nature and its impact on our spiritual growth. I'll share my experiences of finding solace and inspiration in the great outdoors, and how these moments have taught me to embrace my inner light. We'll also uncover ways to tap into the Earth's energy so you can experience the tranquility and empowerment that nature provides.

But the journey doesn't end there, sis! We'll also dive into the significance of our tribe – the people who cheer us on, share our laughter and tears, and help us grow into the phenomenal women we were destined to be. We'll discuss the importance of surrounding ourselves with positive, like-minded individuals who understand our journey and support our growth.

Together, we'll learn to appreciate the beauty of our surroundings, and the people who make life worth living. By the end of this chapter, you'll have a renewed sense of appreciation for the world around you and the tribe that nurtures your spirit. So, take a deep breath, and let's dive into the extraordinary world of connections, healing, and empowerment that awaits us!

## THE HEALING POWER OF NATURE

Now, I want to share a story about my dear friend Maya. On the surface, she appeared to have it all: a thriving career, a beautiful family, and an infectious laugh that could light up a room. But deep down, she was grappling with the weight of life's demands, leaving her feeling overwhelmed and disconnected from her true self.

One day, feeling particularly frazzled, Maya decided to take a much-needed break and ventured out to a nearby park. As she strolled along the winding paths, breathing in the fresh air and taking in the vibrant colors of the surrounding foliage, something incredible happened. She felt a profound sense of calm wash over her, and with each step, she could feel her worries and stress melting away.

Over time, Maya made it a point to incorporate nature walks into her self-care routine, and she noticed a remarkable shift in her overall well-being. She found that spending time in nature helped her reconnect with her inner self, regain a sense of balance, and cultivate inner peace.

Just like Maya, you too can experience the transformative connection with the earth by incorporating nature into your self-care practice.

So, let's talk about how spending time in nature can help you reduce stress. Picture yourself surrounded by lush greenery, the gentle sounds of birds singing, and the soothing sight of a flowing stream. It's no surprise that our bodies and minds begin to relax in this environment. This relaxation helps lower cortisol levels, improving our immune systems and overall well-being.

## Tuning In and Getting in Touch

Nature also allows us to tune in and get in touch with our inner selves. Away from the noise and distractions of our daily lives, we can find clarity and focus, helping us understand our needs, desires, and aspirations better. Embrace the magic of sunrises and the wisdom of ancient trees, feeling the vibrations of the earth beneath our feet, and finding solace in the whispers of the wind. When we know ourselves better, we can make more informed choices that lead to more fulfilling lives.

## Cultivating Gratitude through Nature

Connecting with nature can also foster a sense of gratitude and appreciation for the world around us. When you take a moment to marvel at the beauty of a sunset, the intricacy of a flower, or the graceful flight of a bird, you are reminded of the countless blessings that surround you every day. Cultivating gratitude can help shift your perspective and find joy in even the simplest things.

## Incorporating Nature into Your Daily Routine

So, how can you embrace the healing power of nature? Start by making it part of your daily routine. Set aside time each day to get outside and immerse yourself in your natural surroundings. Whether it's a morning walk around your neighborhood, a lunch break in the park, or an evening stroll through a nearby nature reserve, consistency is key to forming a deep connection with the natural world.

### Mindfulness and Meditation in Nature

Another way to connect with nature is through mindfulness and meditation. When you're outside, take a few moments to focus on your breath and become present in the moment. Engage all your senses: feel the breeze on your skin, hear the birds singing, and smell the scent of the earth. By engaging in outdoor self-care practices, like forest bathing and moonlit meditation, we can reconnect with our roots and find our inner strength.

### Nature-Infused Activities for Deeper Connection

And don't forget about activities that allow you to interact with nature more intimately. Gardening, hiking, or even forest bathing are all fantastic ways to immerse yourself in the natural world and experience its healing benefits firsthand. So, take the time to explore and embrace the healing power of nature, and watch as it works its magic on your mind, body, and soul.

## BUILDING A SUPPORTIVE COMMUNITY

Now that we've explored the healing power of nature, let's jump into how you can build a supportive community. Connecting with others is just as important as connecting with the Earth when it comes to nurturing our souls and advancing on our personal growth journey. In this section, we'll discuss the significance of surrounding ourselves with like-minded individuals and creating a network of support that uplifts and encourages us.

## A Tale of Sisterhood and Support

Allow me to share Tasha's story. Tasha was a dedicated and hard-working single mom who found herself struggling to balance her demanding job, her personal life, and caring for her two children. She often felt overwhelmed and isolated, with no time or energy left for herself. One day, Tasha's coworker invited her to join a local support group for Black women focusing on personal growth and self-care.

Initially, Tasha hesitated, worried about adding one more commitment to her already packed schedule. However, she decided to give it a try, hoping to find a reprieve from her daily stress. Little did she know, this decision would change her life forever.

At the group meetings, Tasha met an amazing circle of women from diverse backgrounds, each with their own struggles and triumphs. As they shared their stories, Tasha realized she wasn't alone in her struggles, and she found solace in their empathy and understanding. The group became a safe space where they could all share their challenges, uplift one another, and work together to create positive change in their lives.

Over time, Tasha's newfound sisterhood provided her with the encouragement and motivation she needed to make essential changes in her life. With their support, she found the strength to pursue a more flexible job, allowing her to have more quality time with her children and dedicate time for self-care. In turn, Tasha became a source of inspiration for the other women in her tribe, empowering them to take charge of their lives and make their own positive changes.

Tasha's story demonstrates the power of sisterhood and the importance of building a supportive community. By surrounding ourselves with like-minded individuals, nurturing these relationships, and engaging in shared experiences, we can create a network of support that uplifts and encourages us to embrace our power and reach our full potential.

## Creating Your Tribe

It's essential to surround yourself with people who understand your goals, aspirations, and values. These individuals will inspire and motivate you to stay on track and pursue your dreams, even when the going gets tough. When seeking out these connections, consider friends, family members, or joining clubs and groups where you'll find people who share your interests and passions. By doing so, you'll create a tribe of strong, supportive, and empowering individuals who genuinely have your back.

## Nurturing Relationships

Nurturing these relationships is a vital aspect of creating a supportive community. You can start by maintaining open lines of communication and sharing your experiences, struggles, and triumphs. This exchange allows your tribe to offer encouragement, advice, and even a shoulder to cry on when needed. By cultivating these connections, you'll find that your tribe becomes a source of strength and inspiration in your personal growth journey.

## Shared Experiences and Celebrations

Another important aspect of building a supportive community is engaging in shared experiences. Participate in activities that bring you closer to your tribe and allow you to bond over common interests. Whether it's attending events, workshops, or simply going for a walk in nature together, these shared experiences will strengthen your connections and create lasting memories. Moreover, fostering a culture of empathy and understanding within your community is crucial. We all face setbacks and challenges, and during these times, we need our tribe to be there for us.

**Expanding and Evolving Your Community**

Finally, remember that building a supportive community is an ongoing process. As you grow and evolve, so will your tribe. Be open to meeting new people and expanding your network to include those who share your vision and values. By doing so, you'll continue to enrich your life and the lives of those around you.

Establishing a supportive community is a vital aspect of personal growth and empowerment for Black women. By surrounding ourselves with like-minded individuals, nurturing these relationships, and engaging in shared experiences, we can create a network of support that uplifts and encourages us to embrace our power and reach our full potential.

## ENGAGING IN OUTDOOR SELF-CARE PRACTICES

Having explored building a supportive community, let's dive into the wonders of outdoor self-care practices. Engaging with nature is not only a beautiful way to practice self-care but also a fantastic opportunity to connect with your tribe and share meaningful experiences. In this section, we'll explore various outdoor activities you can incorporate into your self-care routine while discussing their numerous benefits.

First, let's talk about the magic of walking. Walking outdoors, whether it's in a park, along a trail, or just around your neighborhood, is a simple yet powerful way to clear your mind, get some exercise, and enjoy the beauty of nature. As you stroll, take time to notice the sounds, sights, and smells around you, allowing them to soothe your senses and rejuvenate your spirit. Invite your tribe to join you, turning your walk into a bonding experience and an opportunity to share your thoughts and feelings.

Another fantastic outdoor self-care practice is meditation. I can't emphasize enough how transformative meditation can be. Find a quiet, serene spot outside where you can comfortably sit or lay down, close your eyes, and focus on your breath. Allow the natural sounds of your environment to lull you into a state of deep relaxation, letting go of any stress or tension you may be holding onto. As you meditate, visualize yourself releasing any negativity and inhaling the positive, healing energy of nature.

Don't forget the healing power of water, honey. Spending time near bodies of water, such as oceans, lakes, or rivers, can be incredibly therapeutic. Water has a calming effect on our minds and bodies, helping to wash away negative emotions and bring balance to our spirits. Whether you choose to take a dip, stroll along the shoreline, or simply sit and watch the waves, water-based activities are a fantastic way to practice self-care and connect with the Earth.

Gardening is another outdoor self-care practice that can bring joy and a sense of accomplishment. Tending to plants and watching them grow is not only a form of therapy but also a beautiful metaphor for personal growth. Plus, you get to enjoy the fruits (or veggies) of your labor, providing nourishment for both your body and soul. Invite your tribe to join you in creating a community garden, fostering connection and support as you nurture life together.

Lastly, consider participating in outdoor exercise classes or activities with your tribe. From yoga and tai chi to group hikes and dance sessions, engaging in physical activities outdoors is an excellent way to boost your mood, improve your fitness, and strengthen your bonds with your community. As you move your body, allow the fresh air and natural surroundings to energize and uplift your spirit.

As you engage in these outdoor self-care practices, remember to stay present and appreciate the beauty of nature. Use these moments to reflect on your journey, your growth, and your connection with the Earth and your tribe. Embrace the healing power of nature and the love and support of your community as you continue on your path to personal growth, self-love, and empowerment.

Incorporating outdoor self-care practices into your routine is an essential aspect of nurturing your mind, body, and soul. By engaging in activities such as walking, meditating, spending time near water, gardening, and participating in outdoor exercise, you can harness the healing power of nature and foster deeper connections with both the Earth and your tribe. Remember, you deserve to prioritize your self-care and create a life that is abundant, joyful, and fulfilling.

## SUMMARY, ACTION STEPS & EXERCISES

- Schedule regular outdoor self-care activities: Set aside time each week to engage in activities that connect you with nature, like taking a walk in the park, hiking, or gardening. Embrace the peace and tranquility of the natural world to nourish your soul and recharge your energy.
- Foster connections with like-minded individuals: Reach out to friends, family, or local groups who share your interests in nature and self-care. Plan outdoor activities together, such as picnics or nature walks, to create a supportive and nurturing community.
- Practice mindfulness during outdoor activities: As you spend time in nature, consciously tune into your senses, taking in the sights, sounds, and smells around you. This mindful approach will deepen your connection

with the earth and enhance the healing benefits of your outdoor experiences.

---

Throughout this chapter, we've journeyed together through the healing power of nature and the importance of building a supportive community to uplift and sustain us.

As we move forward in our journey of self-care mastery, it's time to delve into another essential aspect of our lives: the sacred relationship between spirituality and sexuality. By uniting these two powerful forces, we can tap into our divine feminine power, ignite our inner goddess, and embrace our wholeness as Black women.

In the next chapter, we'll explore the connection between our spiritual and sexual selves, learning ways to harmonize these energies and deepen our understanding of our divine femininity. We'll unlock the secrets of sacred sexuality, experience the transformative power of Tantra, and discover how to channel our sexual energy to manifest our dreams and desires.

So, stay with me on this beautiful journey of self-discovery, sis! Let's continue to unlock our power, reclaim our lives, and embrace the abundance that awaits us. Together, we are unstoppable! By nurturing our connection to nature, our tribe, and our divine femininity, we will continue to flourish and grow as strong, radiant Black women. Let's keep moving forward, hand in hand, on this incredible journey of self-love, growth, and empowerment, as we write our own unique stories and celebrate our magic.

# CHAPTER 10
# DIVINE FEMININITY: UNITING SPIRITUALITY AND SEXUALITY

"THERE IS NO FORCE MORE POWERFUL THAN A WOMAN DETERMINED TO RISE." - W.E.B. DU BOIS

H ave you ever considered the profound connection between our sexuality and spirituality? For many Black women, society has taught us to suppress our sexuality, but the truth is, it's an essential component of our spiritual journey. In this chapter, we're going to uncover the beautiful and intricate relationship between spirituality and sexuality, as well as how to harness your divine feminine power.

Prepare to dive deep into the world of spiritual and sexual energy, exploring how to strike a harmonious balance that allows you to thrive in every aspect of your life. We'll also touch on ways to enhance intimacy with your partner through spiritual practices, ultimately empowering you to fully embrace and honor your divine femininity. This journey of self-discovery will not only help you connect with your authentic self, but it will also enable you to form more profound connections with others, transforming your life in ways you never thought possible. So, let's get ready to break free from societal constraints and step into the fullness of our divine, sensual, and spiritual selves.

# THE CONNECTION BETWEEN SPIRITUALITY AND SEXUALITY

Let's talk about the beautiful connection between spirituality and sexuality. Now, I know this might sound like an odd pairing, but trust me, once you see how they intertwine and complement each other, it'll be a lightbulb moment. So, let's dig in and uncover how these powerful energies can transform your life and lead you to a deeper understanding of your divine femininity.

## Recognizing the Connection

First things first, let's acknowledge that spirituality and sexuality aren't separate entities; they're two sides of the same coin, girl. Your spiritual journey and your sensual energy are both essential parts of your divine femininity. When you embrace this connection, you start to harness your full potential as a strong, empowered Black woman.

You remember Keisha, right? Well, she was struggling to feel confident in her skin and often felt disconnected from her true essence. When she finally embraced her spiritual and sexual aspects, her divine feminine energy flourished, and she began to radiate confidence and love from within. You can experience this transformation too, girl!

## Mindfulness and Meditation: Bridging the Gap

If you're wondering how to connect your spiritual and sexual energies, look no further than mindfulness and meditation. Taking a few moments every day to focus on your breath and tune into your body will help you feel more connected to both your spiritual essence and your sensual vitality.

Try meditating with a focus on your sacral chakra, the energy center linked to creativity, sensuality, and emotions. Visualize a warm, orange light glowing in your lower abdomen, representing your divine feminine power. As you breathe in, imagine this light growing brighter, and as you exhale, feel it radiating throughout your entire being.

## Self-Love: The Key to Uniting Your Energies

Girl, I can't stress this enough: self-love is essential when it comes to uniting your spiritual and sexual energies. You need to love and accept yourself unconditionally to create a nurturing environment for both aspects of your divine femininity to thrive. So, be kind to yourself and practice self-compassion because you're deserving of all the love and abundance the universe has to offer.

## Creative Expression: Let Your Soul Soar

Another powerful way to explore the connection between spirituality and sexuality is through creative expression. When you engage in activities that allow you to express your passion, desires, and emotions, you're tapping into your divine feminine power.

So, go ahead and dance like nobody's watching, paint your heart out, or belt out your favorite tune in the shower. Whatever makes your soul soar, girl, do it! You'll find that embracing your creativity will help you connect with your spiritual and sensual sides even more.

## Shanice's Transformation

Let me tell you about my friend Shanice. She felt trapped in her daily routine, feeling like she was missing something crucial in her life. When she began embracing the connection between her spirituality and sexuality, everything changed for her. Shanice found a sense of freedom and empowerment she never knew was possible. By honoring both aspects of her divine femininity, she unlocked her full potential and stepped into her power.

As we wrap up this exploration of the connection between spirituality and sexuality, remember that personal growth is a journey, and it's okay to take it one step at a time. Just like Shanice, you can learn to embrace your divine femininity and experience the transformative power of uniting your spiritual and sensual energies.

In the next section, we'll dive deeper into balancing these energies, discovering more ways to harness their power and bring harmony to your life.

## BALANCING SPIRITUAL AND SEXUAL ENERGY

We've talked about the beautiful connection between spirituality and sexuality, and now it's time to explore how we can balance our spiritual and sexual energy. As Black women, we understand the importance of harmony in our lives, and finding this balance is crucial for our spiritual and sensual selves.

**Self-awareness:** To balance our energies, we need to be aware of them. Take time each day to check in with yourself and notice your emotional, mental, and physical states. Reflect on what you need to achieve balance, whether it's more spiritual practices, like meditation or prayer, or activities that awaken your sensual side, like dancing or self-love rituals.

**Set boundaries:** Knowing when to say "no" is essential for maintaining balance. Set boundaries that honor both your spiritual and sensual selves and be willing to step away from situations or relationships that don't serve your highest good.

**Embrace vulnerability:** Communicate your needs, desires, and fears. This creates space for growth and deeper connections with ourselves and others. Share your thoughts and feelings with a trusted friend, partner, or journal to gain clarity and insight.

**Be mindful of the messages you consume:** The content we engage with can affect our self-perception and relationships. Surround yourself with positive influences that uplift and empower you, from music and books to social media accounts.

**Cultivate sisterhood:** Building a supportive community of like-minded Black women can help you navigate your journey to self-discovery and balance. Connect with others who share your values and can provide encouragement and guidance.

**Practice self-compassion:** Give yourself permission to be a work in progress. Recognize that you may not always feel perfectly balanced and that's okay. Treat yourself with kindness and patience as you work towards harmony between your spiritual and sexual selves.

To help you on this journey, here are a few reflection questions:

- Which activities or practices make me feel spiritually and sexually alive?
- How can I set boundaries to maintain balance in my life?
- In what ways can I embrace vulnerability to deepen my connections with myself and others?
- What messages am I consuming that might be affecting my self-perception and relationships?
- How can I cultivate a supportive sisterhood to help me navigate my journey to self-discovery and balance?
- In what ways can I practice self-compassion during my journey toward balancing spiritual and sexual energy?

Remember, finding balance between our spiritual and sexual energy is an ongoing process. Be patient with yourself and celebrate your progress along the way. As we continue to nurture this balance, we can unlock our full potential, embracing our divine femininity with unstoppable confidence.

Now that we've touched on balancing spiritual and sexual energy, let's get ready to explore enhancing intimacy through spiritual practices. This is where things get really exciting!

## ENHANCING INTIMACY THROUGH SPIRITUAL PRACTICES

Now that we've covered balancing spiritual and sexual energy, let's explore enhancing intimacy through spiritual practices. Trust me, this is where the magic happens! Integrating spiritual energy into intimate relationships creates deeper connections with ourselves and our partners, taking our experiences to new heights.

First, let's talk about the power of intention setting and mindfulness. Before getting intimate, take a moment to set an intention for the experience, like "I want to connect deeply with my partner" or "I want to fully embrace and enjoy my body." Then, during intimate moments, focus on being present. Pay attention to sensations, emotions, and energy flowing through you. This awareness helps you connect more deeply with your body and partner, intensifying pleasure and deepening your bond.

Another wonderful way to enhance intimacy through spiritual practices is by incorporating rituals and meditation into your love life. Set up a sacred space in your bedroom with candles, incense, and soothing music. Try meditating with your partner before getting intimate, focusing on the energy between the two of you. Visualize the love and connection flowing between you, filling the room with light and warmth. This practice can help you both relax, be more present, and deepen your connection.

And don't forget about breathwork, girl! Breath is our life force, and when we consciously control our breath, we can enhance our experiences and connections with others. Try practicing slow, deep breathing with your partner during intimate moments. Sync your breaths, inhaling and exhaling together. You'll be amazed at how this simple act can create a powerful sense of unity and intimacy.

Now, let's get creative with affirmations and communication. Come up with some empowering, love-focused affirmations to recite, either alone or with your partner, like:

- I am deserving of love and pleasure.
- My body is a temple of divine love.
- We are cultivating a deep and passionate connection with each other.
- I am a magnet for healthy, loving relationships that nourish my soul.
- We create a sacred space for our love to grow and flourish.
- I am worthy of giving and receiving love unconditionally.
- Our intimacy is a beautiful dance of spiritual and physical connection.
- I embrace my divine femininity and empower myself in love and relationships.
- We are a powerful team, lifting each other higher and supporting one another.
- I am a radiant being, attracting love and abundance into my life.
- I trust my intuition and inner guidance in my love life.
- Our love is a harmonious blend of spiritual and sensual energy.
- I celebrate my vulnerability and authenticity in my relationships.

- We communicate openly, honestly, and lovingly with each other.
- I am confident in my ability to create and maintain fulfilling relationships.
- Our love is a constant source of inspiration, growth, and joy.

Share experiences, insights, and desires with your partner, so you can explore and grow together, deepening your connection and love.

Engage in self-reflection. Assess how your spiritual growth has influenced your intimate relationships. Are there areas you can still improve? Keep working on yourself and your connections, and you'll witness the magic unfold in your love life.

### A Journey to Deeper Connection

Karina and her partner, Marc, realized that they needed to make some changes in their relationship. They felt disconnected and were looking for ways to enhance their bond. That's when Karina heard about incorporating spiritual practices into their love life. Intrigued by the idea, they both decided to give it a try.

### Creating a Sacred Space

One evening, Karina and Marc transformed their bedroom into a sacred space. They lit candles, burned incense, and played soft, soothing music. This calming atmosphere allowed them both to let go of any stress or distractions from their day and focus solely on their connection.

### Intention Setting and Meditation

Before getting intimate, they sat down and set intentions for their experience together. Karina's intention was to be more present and receptive, while Marc's intention was to be more loving and attentive. They then practiced a short meditation, visualizing their love and energy intertwining and filling the room. This exercise helped them both relax and feel more connected to each other.

## Breathwork and Synchronized Breathing

As they moved into their intimate moments, Karina and Marc tried synchronizing their breaths. They inhaled and exhaled deeply and slowly, consciously matching each other's rhythm. To their surprise, this simple act of breathing together created an incredible sense of unity and intimacy they had never felt before.

## Affirmations and Communication

Karina and Marc also incorporated affirmations into their love life. They chose affirmations that resonated with them, such as "Our love is a harmonious blend of spiritual and sensual energy" and "We communicate openly, honestly, and lovingly with each other." They recited these affirmations together, which helped foster a positive and loving mindset.

## The Results

After several weeks of practicing these spiritual techniques, Karina and Marc noticed a significant shift in their relationship. Their communication improved, and they felt more in tune with each other's emotions and desires. They found that their intimate moments were more passionate and fulfilling, and their bond grew stronger than ever before.

Karina now swears by these practices and continues to explore new ways to blend spirituality and intimacy.

Remember, as you journey through life embracing both spiritual and sexual energy, they're not separate entities but intertwined aspects of your divine femininity. By harmonizing these energies and integrating spiritual practices into your love life, you'll experience deeper connections, increased self-awareness, and newfound empowerment. Shine on!

## SUMMARY, ACTION STEPS & EXERCISES

- Explore your spiritual beliefs around sexuality: Reflect on how your spirituality and sexuality intersect and support one another. Recognize that embracing both aspects can lead to a more fulfilling and balanced life.
- Practice mindful intimacy: During intimate moments with a partner or by yourself, focus on being present and fully experiencing each sensation. This mindful approach can help deepen connections and heighten pleasure.
- Incorporate meditation into your intimate life: Set aside time to meditate on your desires and sexual energy, either alone or with a partner. This practice can help strengthen your connection to your divine feminine energy and enhance your overall well-being.

As we uncovered the connection between spirituality and sexuality in this chapter, it's become clear how integral it is to acknowledge and honor these intertwined aspects of ourselves as Black women.

As you continue on this journey of self-discovery, remember to carry this newfound wisdom with you. Your sexuality and spirituality are sacred parts of who you are and nurturing them in tandem contributes to your overall growth and well-being.

Now, as we progress further in our spiritual self-care journey, it's time to focus on creating an environment that supports your growth and nourishes your soul. In the next chapter, we'll explore how to establish a sacred space within your home - a sanctuary designed to encourage self-care, spiritual connection, and personal growth. Join me, as we move forward together in our journey to unlock our power, reclaim our lives, and embrace abundance with unstoppable confidence.

So, get ready to transform your surroundings and elevate your spiritual self-care experience. With each step we take, we continue to unlock our power, embrace abundance, and move confidently through life as strong, radiant Black women. Embrace your divine femininity, and let's keep flourishing together on this journey of self-love, growth, and empowerment.

# CHAPTER 11
# CREATING A SANCTUARY FOR YOUR SOUL

"YOUR SACRED SPACE IS WHERE YOU CAN FIND YOURSELF AGAIN AND AGAIN." - JOSEPH CAMPBELL

Can you imagine how having a personal sanctuary can have an impact on your spiritual growth and overall well-being? It might seem like a small detail, but having a dedicated space in your home to connect with your higher self can bring a sense of tranquility, balance, and inspiration. In this chapter, we're going to dive into the importance of designing your sacred space, providing tips on how to create a sanctuary that reflects your spiritual essence, and guiding you to incorporate meaningful elements that ignite your soul.

We'll explore the significance of a spiritual sanctuary, the process of designing your own sacred space, and how to include elements that hold deep meaning for you. Discover how to use colors, symbols, and natural elements to create a haven that nurtures your spirit and supports your self-care journey. By the end of this chapter, you'll have a better understanding of the power of a personal sanctuary and how it can serve as a foundation for your spiritual growth, ultimately contributing to a more balanced and fulfilling life.

## THE SIGNIFICANCE OF HAVING A SPIRITUAL SANCTUARY

You know that cozy spot where you can escape from the hustle and bustle of daily life and just be one with yourself? We all need that sanctuary where we can recharge, reflect, and reconnect with our spiritual selves. So, let's explore the significance of crafting a soulful haven.

First and foremost, a spiritual sanctuary offers you a safe space for self-care. It's essential to treat your soul with as much love and attention as your body! A sanctuary is a sacred space where you can release stress, indulge in some well-deserved "me time," and concentrate on your spiritual growth. Trust me, your soul will be eternally grateful for this nurturing environment!

Another benefit of having a spiritual sanctuary is that it allows you to tap into your inner wisdom. When you have a quiet, sacred space to meditate and reflect, you can access your intuition and receive guidance from your higher self. It's like having a direct line to your very own spiritual GPS!

Now, let's talk about the role a spiritual sanctuary plays in fostering a deeper connection with the divine. When you create a sacred space dedicated to spiritual practice, you're sending a powerful message to the universe that you're committed to your spiritual journey. This, in turn, strengthens your connection with the divine and invites more spiritual guidance and blessings into your life.

Before we dive into tips for designing your personal sacred space, let me share a heartfelt story about Dominique. She was going through a particularly rough patch in her life, dealing with a demanding job and a tumultuous relationship. Dominique came to the realization that she needed a haven where she could escape the chaos and concentrate on her spiritual well-being.

So, she took matters into her own hands and created a sanctuary in her home. Dominique began by carving out a small, intimate corner of her bedroom, and filled it with items that held deep meaning for her – crystals, candles, and a vision board showcasing her dreams and aspirations. Every day, she spent precious moments in her sanctuary, meditating, journaling, and reflecting on her life's journey.

Over time, Dominique noticed a remarkable shift in her mental and emotional well-being. She felt more grounded, centered, and better equipped to handle life's challenges. Her sanctuary became her lifeline, a place of solace and empowerment, helping her navigate the rough waters of her life with grace, resilience, and a renewed sense of purpose.

Inspired by her experience, Dominique began to share her story with others, encouraging them to create their own sacred spaces to support their spiritual growth and self-care. Her story serves as a powerful reminder of the impact a personal sanctuary can have on our lives, transforming not only our environment but our very essence as well.

## TIPS FOR DESIGNING YOUR PERSONAL SACRED SPACE

Now that we've discussed the importance of having a spiritual sanctuary, let's dive into the process of designing your personal sacred space and creating an altar. This is where you can unleash your divine femininity and celebrate the perfect union of spirituality and sexuality. Remember, this is your personal sanctuary, so let it be a reflection of your unique spiritual essence.

Building a sanctuary that nurtures your soul is all about including aspects that resonate with you on a personal and spiritual level. By embracing the power of personal touches, colors, textures, aromatherapy, symbols, artwork, and nature, you can create a space that's uniquely yours - filled with love, light, and positive energy.

## Choose Colors and Textures

Think about the colors and textures that will set the atmosphere for your spiritual retreat. Colors significantly influence our mood and energy, so choose shades that uplift and calm your spirit. Complement these colors with textures like plush rugs, soft cushions, or silky fabrics to add depth and warmth to your space.

## Choose a Space

Begin by selecting a spot in your home that feels inviting, peaceful, and private as your sacred space. This space should feel like an extension of your personality, reflecting your unique qualities and spiritual journey. Add personal items that hold special meaning, such as family heirlooms, cherished gifts, or photographs. These elements serve as visual reminders of your values and experiences, fostering a deep connection between you and your sanctuary.

## Set the Atmosphere

Cultivate a calming, peaceful environment with soft lighting or fairy lights to create a warm, inviting glow. Use soothing scents like essential oils or incense, and tranquil music. This ambiance will help ease your transition into a more spiritually attuned state of mind.

Aromatherapy can also play a crucial role in setting the tone and energy of your sacred space. Essential oils, incense, or scented candles create an inviting and comforting atmosphere, allowing you to relax and connect with your inner self. Experiment with fragrances like lavender for relaxation, citrus for invigoration, or sandalwood for grounding. Choose scents that speak to your soul and make you feel good.

## Surround Yourself with Symbols and Artwork

Display symbols and artwork that resonate with your spiritual beliefs and aspirations. Perhaps a beautiful painting of a goddess, a sculpture of an ancestor, or a vibrant tapestry with meaningful patterns. These visual reminders serve as constant sources of inspiration and motivation as you journey through life. Bring a little piece of Mother Earth into your sanctuary by adding plants, crystals, or other natural elements to ground your energy, cleanse the space, and create a sense of harmony and balance.

## Personalize Your Space

Fill your sacred space with items that hold personal meaning and significance for you. Consider crystals, candles, inspiring photos, or spiritual texts that resonate with your beliefs. Be creative and choose items that reflect your unique spiritual journey.

## Create a Comfortable Area for Meditation and Reflection

Design a cozy area with a cushion or soft rug where you can sit or recline during your spiritual practices. You might also want to include a cozy blanket or shawl to wrap yourself in during your time in your sanctuary.

## Celebrate Your Sensuality

Incorporate elements that engage your senses and celebrate your sensuality, such as soft, luxurious fabrics, a sensual playlist, or a collection of erotic literature or art. These elements can help you embrace and express your sensual nature while maintaining a spiritual focus.

## Sound in your sacred space

Soft, soothing music or the gentle sounds of a water fountain can calm the mind and enhance your meditation or relaxation experience. Alternatively, you may prefer silence to help you focus and connect with your inner self.

## Establish a Routine

Commit to spending time in your sanctuary each day, whether it's just 10 minutes or a full hour. This dedicated time will help you create a consistent spiritual practice and deepen your connection to your sacred space.

## Create Privacy and Boundaries

Consider adding curtains, screens, or other barriers to separate your sacred space from the rest of your home. This will help you maintain the sanctity of your sanctuary and create a more focused, intimate atmosphere.

## Keep It Sacred and Evolving

Honor your sanctuary by treating it with the utmost respect, keeping it clean, organized, and free from distractions. As you grow and evolve, update your altar, add new items, or rearrange your space to reflect your ever-changing spiritual and sensual identity.

## Your Space Reflects Your Journey

As you create your beautiful, personalized sacred space and altar, it's essential to remember that it serves as a haven for you to explore and nurture both your spiritual and sensual sides. While incorporating various items and elements can enhance the atmosphere, it's crucial to avoid cluttering the space.

## Allow Your Intention to Guide You

Feel free to change out items to match your intention at the time. Your sacred space is an ever-evolving reflection of your journey, and it's perfectly fine to rearrange or replace objects as your needs and desires shift.

### Trust Your Intuition

Lastly, remember that you don't need to include everything mentioned here. Your sacred space is uniquely yours, and it's essential to listen to your own intuition when designing and decorating your sanctuary. Trust your inner guidance, and allow it to lead you in creating a space that truly resonates with your spirit and nurtures your personal growth.

## THE SOULFUL ART AND MEANING OF CRAFTING AN ALTAR

An altar is the centerpiece of your sacred space and serves as a focal point for your spiritual and sensual practices. It represents the harmonious blend of spirituality and sexuality and is a tangible reminder of your intentions, aspirations, and beliefs. Creating an altar is an essential aspect of building a spiritual sanctuary as it helps you connect with your divine nature and nurture your spiritual growth.

Your altar can be as simple or elaborate as you like, from a small table or shelf to a decorative tray or a dedicated corner of your sacred space. The key is to choose something that feels sacred and personal to you.

When selecting items for your altar, think about what resonates with you. You might include items like crystals, candles, incense, or flowers. Consider adding symbols of femininity and sensuality, such as a goddess statue, a representation of the moon, or even a beautiful piece of lingerie. The possibilities are endless, so be creative and choose items that reflect your unique spiritual journey.

As you grow and evolve in your spiritual practice, your altar should evolve with you. Update it with new items, rearrange your space, and make adjustments as needed to reflect your ever-changing spiritual and sensual identity. By maintaining a dynamic, personalized altar, you'll strengthen your connection to your spiritual journey and enhance the sacred energy within your sanctuary.

## SUMMARY, ACTION STEPS & EXERCISES

- Set an intention for your sacred space by reflecting on the purpose it will serve, whether it's for meditation, relaxation, or self-reflection. Write down your intention and place it in a visible spot within your sanctuary to remind you of its significance.
- Choose a designated area in your home or outdoor space to create your sanctuary. Clear out any clutter and ensure the space is clean and ready for a transformation. Make it a "no distraction zone" by setting boundaries and letting others in your household know that this area is your special place.
- Gather meaningful elements that resonate with your spirit and personalize your sacred space. Consider including items like cherished photographs, inspiring artwork, cozy textures, soothing colors, and calming scents. As you assemble your sanctuary, focus on creating an atmosphere that brings you peace, inspiration, and a sense of connection to your inner self.

We've discovered the transformative power of creating a sacred space for our personal growth and well-being. We delved into the importance of a spiritual sanctuary and shared tips on designing a space that genuinely reflects our unique essence. We also discussed incorporating meaningful elements and the vital role of colors, symbols, and natural elements in crafting a nurturing environment.

As we continue on this beautiful path of spiritual self-care mastery, we will venture through the world of rituals and routines to maintain consistency in your spiritual practices. We'll explore how to create a daily routine that resonates with your soul and supports your growth, allowing you to unlock your power, reclaim your life, and embrace abundance with unstoppable confidence.

In the upcoming chapter, we'll delve into the art of establishing a solid foundation for our spiritual self-care routines. We'll explore personalized morning and evening routines that support your unique needs, aspirations, and spiritual path, and discuss the importance of setting aside time for solitude and introspection.

As strong, radiant Black women, let us continue to uplift ourselves and each other, creating a ripple effect of empowerment and positive change in our communities and beyond. Together, we'll form a sisterhood of support, love, and encouragement. So, get ready to refine your daily practices and reap the rewards of a consistent and nurturing spiritual self-care routine.

# CHAPTER 12
# RITUALS AND ROUTINES: CONSISTENCY IN SPIRITUAL SELF-CARE

"ALMOST EVERYTHING WILL WORK AGAIN IF YOU UNPLUG IT FOR A FEW MINUTES, INCLUDING YOU." - ANNE LAMOTT

Have you ever wondered how some women seem to be consistently glowing, just radiating positive energy and confidence everywhere they go? What's their secret? Well, let me tell you - it's all about consistency in spiritual self-care! In this chapter, we're going to dive into the importance of daily spiritual rituals, learn the ropes of building a self-care routine that works like magic, and uncover ways to adapt and evolve your practices over time. Commitment and consistency are key, and with them, you'll soon find yourself glowing from the inside out, embracing your power, and living your best life.

We're going to explore the fascinating world of rituals and routines, discussing the impact of daily spiritual practices in keeping our emotional and spiritual well-being on point. We'll also dish out some practical tips for creating a self-care routine tailored to your unique needs and preferences. No cookie-cutter routines here, girl!

Plus, we'll delve into how to adapt and evolve your practices over time, making sure your spiritual self-care journey stays fresh, exciting, and oh-so-rewarding. So, get ready to glow, because with the right rituals and routines in place, you'll be shining like the star you are and embracing the limitless possibilities of life!

## THE IMPORTANCE OF DAILY SPIRITUAL RITUALS

Trust me when I say that once you experience the benefits of daily spiritual rituals, you'll wonder how you ever managed without them.

Why are daily spiritual rituals so essential for us as Black women? Well, it's all about connecting with our inner selves, nourishing our souls, and staying grounded amid the chaos of life. We frequently encounter distinct obstacles, and it's crucial that we take the time to care for ourselves, both physically and spiritually. You deserve to feel at peace, empowered, and in tune with your spiritual essence. And guess what? It's easier than you might think.

Let's start by considering my friend Kiyana. She used to be all over the place, feeling stressed and disconnected from herself. But then she started integrating daily spiritual rituals into her life, and let me tell you, it was like night and day! She became more centered, focused, and even seemed to glow with a newfound inner radiance. And that's what I want for you, too.

Now, I'm not suggesting you become a full-blown yogi or spend hours in deep contemplation every day. But incorporating some simple practices into your everyday routine can do wonders for your soul. Let's explore a few straightforward yet powerful practices to help you stay connected to your spirit.

First, consider starting your day with meditation. This practice is all about clearing your mind and connecting with your innermost thoughts and feelings. Even just a few minutes each morning can help relieve stress and give you the clarity you need to tackle the day ahead. Find a quiet space where you can sit comfortably, close your eyes, and focus on your breath. Let any worries or distractions fade away as you become present in the moment. Meditation is like a soothing balm for your soul, giving you the chance to reset and recharge before facing the world.

Next, let's talk about affirmations. Our words have power, so speak life into yourself, sis! Use positive affirmations to uplift and motivate yourself, reminding you of your strength and resilience. Write down a few personal affirmations that resonate with your goals and values and recite them each day. Whether you say them in front of the mirror, in your car, or just in your head, this practice can transform your mindset and boost your confidence.

Now that we've touched on the importance of daily spiritual rituals, it's time to discuss building a self-care routine that works for you. Remember, there's no one-size-fits-all approach when it comes to self-care. You need to find what resonates with you and fits into your unique lifestyle.

Start by carving out some "me time" in your schedule. It might be as simple as waking up a few minutes earlier or setting aside time in the evening to unwind. Dedicate this time to activities that nourish your soul and help you connect with your inner self.

Next, think about the activities that bring you joy and peace. It could be anything from journaling and reading to dancing and taking long walks. Incorporate these activities into your self-care routine, and don't be afraid to mix things up. Variety is the spice of life, after all!

Finally, be gentle with yourself. Rome wasn't built in a day, and neither is a solid self-care routine. It takes time and consistency to see the benefits, so be patient and stay committed. And remember, even small steps in the right direction can make a significant impact on your overall well-being.

Daily spiritual rituals and a personalized self-care routine can help you navigate the adversity we often experience. By dedicating time and effort to nurturing your spirit, you'll find that you're better equipped to tackle life's hurdles with grace and confidence. So go on, embrace the power of rituals and routines, and watch as your life transforms before your eyes.

## BUILDING A SELF-CARE ROUTINE THAT WORKS FOR YOU

Having covered the importance of daily spiritual rituals, let's dive into building a self-care routine that works for you. Remember, your self-care routine is your personal journey, and it should be tailored to your unique needs and preferences. So, grab a pen and paper, and let's get started on creating a routine that will nourish your soul and empower you to be your best self.

First things first, take notice of your current self-care habits. What activities or practices are already working for you? Which ones aren't serving you anymore? Be honest with yourself and identify areas where you can improve. Once you've done this, you'll have a better understanding of what you need to focus on moving forward.

One essential component of a successful self-care routine is setting clear intentions. Ask yourself, "What do I want to achieve through this spiritual practice?" Perhaps you want to cultivate more inner peace, develop a deeper sense of self-love, or simply maintain a positive mindset. Whatever your goals may be, having a clear intention will help guide your journey and keep you focused on what truly matters.

As you build your routine, be sure to incorporate activities that resonate with your spirit and help you connect with your higher self. This might include meditation, journaling, prayer, or spending time in nature. Feel free to mix and match different practices and try new things. The beauty of spiritual self-care is that it's a deeply personal journey, and what works for one person may not work for another. So, don't hesitate to explore different practices and find the ones that truly resonate with your soul.

As you create your self-care routine, it's essential to be gentle with yourself and remember that progress takes time. You might feel more connected and inspired on some days more than others, and that's okay. Embrace the ebb and flow of your spiritual journey, and don't be too hard on yourself if you stumble along the way. As Maya Angelou said, "You may not control all the events that happen to you, but you can decide not to be reduced by them."

One powerful way to stay accountable and committed to your self-care routine is by connecting with other like-minded sisters. Surround yourself with a supportive community of women who uplift and empower each other. Share your experiences, your struggles, and your triumphs, and watch as you grow together in love and sisterhood. As they say, "Iron sharpens iron, and one person sharpens another."

Now, let's talk about adapting and evolving your practices over time. As you journey through life, your needs and priorities will naturally change. It's crucial to remain flexible and open to growth, recognizing that your self-care routine may need to evolve along with you. Be willing to let go of practices that no longer serve you and embrace new ones that resonate with your current circumstances.

When you're feeling stuck or in need of inspiration, don't be afraid to seek guidance from trusted mentors or spiritual teachers. There's a wealth of wisdom available to you, and tapping into others' experiences can provide valuable insights and fresh perspectives.

Building a self-care routine that works for you is a beautiful and empowering journey of self-discovery. As you embark on this path, remember to be consistent, intentional, and open to growth. Surround yourself with a supportive community and never forget that you are a powerful, radiant being capable of overcoming any obstacle that life throws your way. Embrace your spiritual self-care practice with an open heart, and watch as you unlock your power, reclaim your life, and embrace abundance with unstoppable confidence.

## ADAPTING AND EVOLVING YOUR PRACTICES OVER TIME

Now that we've talked about building a self-care routine that works for you, it's crucial to discuss the importance of adapting and evolving your practices over time. Just like life, your spiritual journey is ever-changing, and it's essential to keep up with your growth and new experiences. In this section, we'll explore how to maintain flexibility and openness to change in your spiritual self-care routine, allowing you to stay aligned with your evolving needs and priorities.

First and foremost, embracing change is a vital aspect of personal growth. As you progress in your spiritual journey, you may notice that your needs, priorities, and interests shift. These changes can be attributed to various factors, including personal development, life experiences, and new perspectives. It's essential to remember that change is a sign of growth and evolution, so don't be afraid to welcome it with open arms. Letting go of practices that no longer resonate with you allows you to make space for new ones that better align with your current state of being.

To stay in tune with your evolving self, it's important to reflect on your needs and progress regularly. This reflection can take the form of journaling, meditating, or simply taking some time to sit quietly and think about your spiritual journey. By evaluating your current practices and considering how they're serving you, you can identify areas where change is necessary. Regular reflection also allows you to celebrate your achievements and progress, providing motivation to continue moving forward on your spiritual path.

Another key aspect of adapting and evolving your spiritual self-care routine is staying open to new experiences and practices. There's a vast array of spiritual practices and traditions available to explore, each with its unique benefits and insights. Keep an open mind and be willing to try new things, as you may discover a practice that speaks to you on a deeper level. Connecting with others on their spiritual journey can also provide inspiration, as their experiences and insights can help expand your perspective.

As you incorporate new practices and make changes to your spiritual self-care routine, it's essential to maintain balance. While it's beneficial to explore new methods and adjust, it's also important not to overwhelm yourself with too many changes at once. Gradually implementing new practices and allowing yourself time to adjust will help maintain a sense of balance and prevent burnout.

Lastly, remember that your spiritual self-care journey is unique to you. What works for someone else may not necessarily resonate with you, and that's okay. Trust your intuition and listen to your inner guidance when making changes to your routine. By staying true to yourself and honoring your personal journey, you'll be able to create a spiritual self-care practice that evolves and adapts alongside you.

Adapting and evolving your spiritual self-care practices over time is essential for maintaining alignment with your ever-changing needs and priorities. By embracing change, reflecting on your progress, staying open to new experiences, and maintaining balance, you can ensure that your spiritual self-care routine continues to support and nourish you throughout.

## SUMMARY, ACTION STEPS & EXERCISES

- Start each day with a simple spiritual ritual that brings you peace, such as morning meditation, prayer, or gratitude journaling. Make it a non-negotiable part of your daily routine.
- Identify activities that replenish your energy and prioritize them in your daily life. This can include exercise, spending time in nature, or engaging in creative hobbies. Create a self-care routine that works for you and commit to it.
- Stay open to adapting and evolving your practices over time as your needs and circumstances change. Don't be afraid to try new things or adjust your routine to better support your growth and well-being. Remember, self-care is a journey, and it's all about finding what works best for you.

---

Girl, we've come such a long way together in this spiritual self-care journey, and I couldn't be prouder of you! In this chapter, we delved deep into the importance of rituals and routines, exploring how they form the backbone of a consistent spiritual self-care practice.

Throughout this chapter, we discovered the impact of daily spiritual rituals on our overall well-being. These rituals, whether it's meditation, journaling, or prayer, play a vital role in keeping us grounded, connected to our inner selves, and growing on a personal and spiritual level. As Black women, we need these daily rituals to support us in facing life's challenges head-on and with unwavering resilience.

Remember, consistency is key to unlocking the full power of spiritual self-care in your life. So, go on – make those rituals and routines work for you! Your journey doesn't end here; it's just the beginning. Keep exploring, learning, and growing, and know that I'm rooting for you every step of the way.

# CHAPTER 13

# VIBRANT VITALITY: NOURISHING YOUR MIND, BODY, AND SPIRIT

*"Self-care is never a selfish act—it is simply good stewardship of the only gift I have, the gift I was put on earth to offer to others." - Parker J. Palmer*

Are you ready to unlock the powerful synergy between your mind, body, and spirit, sis? It's a fact that when we care for every aspect of ourselves, we not only improve our physical health but also empower ourselves to live more vibrant and fulfilling lives. In this chapter, we'll explore how holistic wellness is an essential part of your spiritual self-care journey. We'll discuss the importance of nutritional and lifestyle choices that support your spiritual growth and overall well-being. By learning techniques to maintain balance and energy flow, you'll achieve optimal well-being and fully embrace the interconnectedness of your mind, body, and spirit.

Throughout this chapter, we'll examine the significance of holistic wellness and how it impacts your spiritual self-care journey. We'll provide you with valuable insights on making informed nutritional and lifestyle choices that align with your spiritual growth. Additionally, we'll cover techniques that help maintain balance and energy flow, ultimately leading to optimal well-being and a greater sense of empowerment. So, let's embark on this journey of nourishment and growth, and unleash the vibrant vitality within you!

## THE IMPORTANCE OF HOLISTIC WELLNESS IN YOUR SPIRITUAL SELF-CARE JOURNEY

Girl, let me tell you, holistic wellness is the key to unlocking the best version of yourself. Now, I know it might sound like a cliché, but trust me when I say that taking care of your mind, body, and spirit is essential in our spiritual self-care journey. It's time to step up and nurture every aspect of your being, sis! So let's dive into the importance of holistic wellness in your spiritual self-care journey.

First off, let's talk about the mind. You know as well as I do that our mental well-being is just as important as our physical health. As we've discussed, we often deal with a lot – from microaggressions to more significant societal pressures. But you know what? We're strong, resilient, and capable of overcoming these challenges. To keep our minds sharp and healthy, it's essential to practice mindfulness, meditation, and engage in activities that stimulate our brains.

Speaking of meditation, let's not forget about our spiritual well-being. Connecting with a higher power or simply finding a sense of inner peace and purpose can make a world of difference in our lives. It's like that one time my girl Shaniqua started attending a meditation group at her local community center. She went from being stressed and overwhelmed to feeling calm, focused, and more connected to her inner self. And that shift in her energy was contagious! It's crucial for us to find practices that resonate with our souls, whether it's prayer, meditation, or even spending time in nature.

Now let's move on to the physical aspect of holistic wellness. Your body is your temple, so it's essential to treat it with love and respect. Regular exercise, adequate sleep, and stress management are all critical components of maintaining a healthy body. And when you take care of your body, your mind and spirit will thank you for it, too.

As you embark on this journey towards holistic wellness, take some time to reflect on your current habits and routines. Ask yourself: What areas of my life can I improve to achieve a better balance between my mind, body, and spirit? What steps can I take to nurture every aspect of my being? Remember, self-reflection is essential for personal growth and self-awareness.

Holistic wellness is a crucial component of our spiritual self-care journey. By nurturing our minds, bodies, and spirits, we can unlock our full potential and step into our power. So go ahead, girl – take care of yourself, embrace your vibrant vitality, and show the world what you're made of!

## NUTRITIONAL AND LIFESTYLE CHOICES THAT SUPPORT YOUR SPIRITUAL GROWTH

Now that we've talked about the importance of holistic wellness in your spiritual self-care journey, let's discuss the nutritional and lifestyle choices that can support your spiritual growth. it's time to show your body some love and make choices that'll nourish you inside and out!

**Mindful Eating:** The food we eat can affect not only our physical health but also our mental and spiritual well-being. So, let's get intentional about what we put into our bodies. Focus on consuming whole, nutrient-dense foods that provide the vitamins and minerals your body needs. Remember that saying, "You are what you eat"? Well, it's time to become a whole, vibrant, and nourished queen.

**Hydration is Key:** Don't underestimate the power of water! Staying hydrated keeps our bodies functioning at their best, plus it helps flush out toxins and maintain our energy levels. Aim for at least eight glasses a day, and if you want to make it more fun, add some fruit slices or herbs for a flavorful twist!

**Get Moving:** Exercise is essential for our physical, mental, and spiritual well-being. Find activities that you enjoy, like dancing, yoga, or even just walking around the block. Moving your body regularly helps release feel-good endorphins, reduces stress, and keeps you feeling strong and empowered.

**Prioritize Sleep:** As busy Black women, we often sacrifice sleep for the sake of getting things done. But getting enough sleep is vital for our overall health and well-being. Make it a priority to get at least seven hours of quality sleep each night and watch how your energy and mood improve.

**Manage Stress:** Stress can have a significant impact on our bodies and spirits. Find healthy ways to cope with life's challenges, such as meditation, journaling, or even talking to a trusted friend or therapist. Remember, it's okay to ask for help and support when you need it.

Cultivate a Supportive Environment: Surround yourself with positive energy and people who uplift and inspire you. Create a space at home that brings you peace and joy. This might mean decluttering, adding plants, or using calming scents like lavender or eucalyptus.

Now, take a moment to reflect on your current nutritional and lifestyle habits. What changes can you make to better support your spiritual growth? Write down your thoughts and create a plan to implement these changes in your life.

As you start making these nutritional and lifestyle choices, you'll notice a shift in your energy and well-being. Your mind, body, and spirit will thank you for taking care of yourself in this way.

Up next, let's dive into techniques to maintain balance and energy flow for optimal well-being. Trust me, once you master these techniques, you'll feel unstoppable on your journey to self-love and empowerment. So, let's keep going and explore more ways to nourish your vibrant vitality!

## TECHNIQUES TO MAINTAIN BALANCE AND ENERGY FLOW FOR OPTIMAL WELL-BEING

Now that we've spoken about the nutritional and lifestyle choices that support your spiritual growth, let's explore techniques to maintain balance and energy flow for optimal well-being. As Black women, we experience life's ups and downs in our unique ways, but we got this! Let's dive into some powerful techniques to keep you shining bright.

**Grounding:** Connecting with the earth is a powerful way to maintain balance and stability. Spend time in nature, walk barefoot on the grass, or simply visualize yourself rooted to the earth. Let Mother Nature's energy help you stay grounded, sis.

**Meditation:** This ancient practice is a game-changer when it comes to balancing our energy. Set aside some time each day to quiet your mind and connect with your inner self. Experiment with different meditation styles to find the one that resonates with you.

**Breathwork:** Our breath is our life force, so let's use it to our advantage! Practice deep, mindful breathing to release tension and stress, and to center yourself. Try inhaling for a count of four, holding for four, and exhaling for a count of six. You'll be amazed at how this simple technique can transform your energy.

**Chakra Balancing:** Our chakras are energy centers that govern different aspects of our lives. When they're in balance, we feel vibrant and aligned. Explore practices like yoga, reiki, or sound therapy to balance and align your chakras.

**Emotional Release:** Holding onto negative emotions can weigh us down and block our energy flow. Make space for emotional release through journaling, talking to a trusted friend, or engaging in creative expression like painting or dancing.

**Affirmations and Visualization:** Our thoughts and words have power, girl! Speak life into your dreams and desires by reciting daily affirmations and visualizing yourself achieving your goals. See yourself living in harmony and watch it manifest.

Take a moment to reflect on which techniques resonate with you the most. Consider how you can incorporate them into your daily routine to maintain balance and harmony in your life. Remember, this journey is all about finding what works for you and making it your own.

Being intentional about maintaining balance and energy flow is essential for our overall well-being. As women of color, we deserve to live our lives with a sense of inner peace and confidence. So, let's make a commitment to ourselves to practice these techniques and nurture our mind, body, and spirit.

Keep shining, keep growing, and remember that you are worthy of all the love, abundance, and happiness that life has to offer. Stay connected to your inner strength and wisdom, and watch your life transform into the beautiful masterpiece it's meant to be.

## SUMMARY, ACTION STEPS & EXERCISES

- Whip up a nutritious, soul-nourishing meal: Treat your body with love by preparing a delicious and healthy meal that supports your spiritual growth. Choose colorful fruits, vegetables, and lean protein sources to fuel your mind, body, and spirit.
- Set a daily meditation practice: Carve out 10-15 minutes each day to sit still, focus on your breath, and connect with your inner self. Use this time to release stress and bring harmony to your life.
- Create a personalized energy-balancing routine: Combine grounding, breathwork, chakra balancing, and emotional release techniques to craft a custom routine that works for you. Dedicate time each day to practice these techniques and maintain your vibrant vitality.

In this chapter, we delved deeper into the concept of holistic wellness and its importance in our spiritual self-care journey. We learned that to truly nurture ourselves and support our spiritual growth, we must understand the connection between our mind, body, and spirit. Recognizing this interconnectedness allows us to make informed decisions about our nutritional choices and lifestyle habits, leading to a more fulfilling and balanced life.

Embracing holistic wellness is essential for black women on their spiritual self-care journeys. By understanding the connection between our minds, bodies, and spirits, and making informed nutritional choices, adopting supportive lifestyle habits, and learning energy balancing techniques, we can unlock our power, reclaim our lives, and embrace abundance with unstoppable confidence.

# CONCLUSION

*"Believe in yourself and all that you are. Know that there is something inside you that is greater than any obstacle."*
*— Christian D. Larson*

Can you believe it? We've made it to the end of this incredible spiritual self-care journey together, and let me just say, I am beyond proud of you for sticking with it. I hope by now, you've come to recognize the fierce, unstoppable force that you are – a divine being overflowing with power, wisdom, and resilience. In the words of the one and only Queen Bey herself, "I'm a grown woman, I can do whatever I want" – and that includes taking care of your spirit, mind, and body, sis!

As we close this transformative chapter, let's pause and reflect on the precious gems we've unearthed throughout our journey. We've delved into awakening our spiritual essence, embracing forgiveness, harnessing gratitude, and diving headfirst into the world of mindfulness. Together, we've explored powerful tools that have enabled us to unlock our true potential. We've learned to align our actions with our purpose, discovered the transformative art of yoga, and uncovered the importance of journaling, affirmations, and connecting with nature. And how could we forget about honoring our divine femininity, creating sacred spaces, and building consistent spiritual self-care rituals?

As Black women, we regularly confront hurdles every single day - from systemic barriers to the burden of cultural expectations. It's a heavy load to bear, but we cannot allow it to dim our light. This is where spiritual self-care swoops in to save the day. By nurturing our spirit and prioritizing our well-being, we become better equipped to navigate these challenges and unlock our true potential. Remember, you're never alone in this journey. Our strength and resilience have carried us through generations, and as we tap into the power within us, we rise together.

Having a supportive community can make all the difference, and I know this from personal experience. That's why I want to extend a personal invitation for you to join our YouTube channel, Ambitious Growth Queens. This space is dedicated to providing you with the tools, resources, and inspiration to help you stay on track with your spiritual self-care. By connecting with like-minded sisters, we can uplift each other, share our stories, and continue growing together.

Your journey doesn't end with this book, honey; it's just the beginning.

Now, before I send you off to conquer the world, let me share a little story about my cousin, Kassandra. One day, she found herself struggling to put together a piece of furniture (those IKEA instructions, am I right?). Frustrated and on the verge of tears, she called me for help. When I arrived, I didn't see a defeated woman ready to give up. Instead, I saw a determined, powerful sister who just needed a little encouragement and guidance.

As we worked together, Kassandra began to apply the spiritual self-care principles we've talked about. She took deep breaths, practiced mindfulness, and tapped into her inner strength. And you know what? She managed to assemble that furniture like a pro! It might seem like a small victory, but it was a testament to the power of spiritual self-care in our everyday lives.

Now, I know putting together a bookshelf isn't quite on the same level as conquering life's challenges, but the point is, when we nurture our spirits and believe in ourselves, we can handle anything life throws our way. So, channel your inner Kassandra and face your obstacles head-on, equipped with the spiritual self-care tools you've learned throughout this journey.

As you continue to move forward, always remember that spiritual self-care is an ongoing practice. Keep exploring, learning, and growing, and don't be afraid to adapt and evolve as you journey on. Surround yourself with a tribe of like-minded sisters who uplift and support you, and always remember to uplift and support them too.

You have the power to reclaim your life, embrace abundance, and walk through this world with unstoppable confidence. It's time to take everything you've learned and put it into action. As my girl Maya Angelou said, "Nothing will work unless you do."

So, go out there and show the world what you're made of! Remember, you've got this, and I'm rooting for you every step of the way.

Sending you love, light, and endless encouragement,

With love and light,

Jada Amari

# REFERENCES

Winter M.F. (August 1, 2019). Demystifying Internalized Oppression: The Pain of Internalized oppression. The Inclusion Solution. http://www.theinclusion solution.me/demystifying-internalized-oppression-the-pain-of-internalized-oppression-biases-self-reflection/

Robbins T. The Secrets of Solving Disagreements In Relationships. Tony Robbins. https://www.tonyrobbins.com/ultimate-relationship-guide/resolve-conflict-save-relationship/

Dr. Cloud H. and Dr. Townsend J. (1992). Boundaries. Zondervan.

Earnshaw E. (December 13, 2022). 6 Types of Boundaries You Deserve to Have (and how to maintain them). MBG Relationships. https://www.mindbody green.com/articles/six-types-of-boundaries-and-what-healthy-boundaries-look-like-for-each

Asare J.G. (May 31, 2019). Overcoming the Angry Black Woman Stereotypes. Forbes. https://www.forbes.com/sites/janicegassam/2019/05/31/overcom ing-the-angry-black-woman-stereotype/?sh=6f1a55a91fce

Community Tool Box. Cultural Competence: Healing from Internalized Oppression. Chapter 27. https://ctb.ku.edu/en/table-of-contents/culture/cultural-competence/healing-from-interalized-oppression/main

Jenkins S. (April 28, 2010). EMDR: A Symptom-Based Eight-Phased Treatment. Good Therapy. https://www.goodtherapy.org/blog/emdr-a-symptom-based-eight-phased-treatment/amp/

Mayoclinic Staff (December 13, 2022).    Post Traumatic Stress Disorder. Mayoclinic. https://www.mayoclinic.org/diseases-conditions/post-traumatic-stress-disorder/symptoms-causes/syc-20355967

Moreno R. (August 11, 2022). What Is Body Positivity, and What Does It Mean In 2022?. Oprah Daily. https://www.oprahdaily.com/life/health/a40809665/what-is-body-positivity/

Eaton J. (June 3, 2020). What Black Women Should Know About Building Generational Wealth. Business Insider.    https://www.businessinsider.com/personal-finance/what-want-black-women-know-about-building-genera tional-wealth-2020-6?r=US&IR=T

Herman A. And Murren H. (February 3, 2021). Invest In Black Women to Drive the Economy Forward. Fortune. https://fortune.com/2021/02/03/black-women-economy-diversity-equity-inclusion/amp/

Stanborough R.J. (November 25, 2020). What to Know About a Negative Body Image and How to Overcome It. Healthline. https://www.healthline.com/health/negative-body-image#signs-and-symptoms

Rosenfield J. (June 24, 2022). 8 Real Ways to Multiply Your Money. Yahoo Finance. https://finance.yahoo.com/news/8-real-ways-multiply-money-180045477.html

Taylor S.R. (2008). The Body Is Not An Apology: The Power of Radical Self-Love. Berrett-Koehler Publishers, Inc.

Dr. Lewis V. (2012). Positive Bodies: Loving the Skin You're In. Australian Academic Press.

Washington P. C. Real Money Answers for Every Woman: How to Win the Money Game With or Without a Man.

Hollis R. (2019). Girl, Stop Apologizing: Shame-Free Plan for Embracing and Achieving Your Goals. Harper Collins Leadership.

(September/October 1986). Black Women Face The 21st Century: Major Issues and Problems. The Black Scholar 17(5). Page 12.

Frye J. (August 22, 2029). Racism and Sexism Combine to Shortchange Black Women. The American Progress. https://www.americanprogress.org/article/racism-sexism-combine-shortchange-working-black-women/

Kher S. (November 28, 2018) 10 Practical Tips for Women In the Corporate World. LinkedIn. https://www.linkedin.com/pulse/10-practical-tips-women-corporate-world-suman-kher

Amara H. (2017). Awaken Your Inner Fire. Heirophant Publishing.

McKay M., Forsyth J.P., and Eifert G. H. (2010). Your Life On Purpose: How to Find What Matters, Create the Life You Want. New Harbinger Publications, Inc.

Villarosa L. (August 14, 2019). Myths About Physical Racial Differences. The New York Times. https://www.nytimes.com/interactive/2019/08/14/magazine/racial-differences-doctors.html

Johnson V.E. and Carter R.T. (December 3, 2019). Black Cultural Strength and Psychological Well-Being: An Empirical Analysis with Black American Adults. The Association of Black Psychologists 46(1).

Jim Scott. (2017). Radical Candour: How to Get What You Want By Saying What You Mean. St. Martin's Press.

Bryant S.L. The Beauty Ideal: The Effects of European Standards of Beauty on Black Women. Columbia Social Work Review IV.